"Colonel Studdard explains the lessons in leadership and life learned during a varied and demanding Marine Corps career at both war and peace and translates them effectively into valuable insights for business leaders and transitioning individuals. His journey from Marine private to Marine colonel is inspiring; it's marked by his and his family's dedicated service and sacrifice and his service under brilliant Marines who set the example, fostered his talents and taught him life lessons. An inspiring read!"

—Lieutenant General Richard Mills, USMC (Ret),
President and Chief Executive Officer, Marine Corps
University Foundation

"There are two standing orders for a leader of Marines: accomplish the mission and take care of your Marines. United States Marine (Retired) Colonel Ted Studdard did exactly that during a Marine Corps career that took him from private to colonel and spanned both combat and peace time duties.

"From multiple combat tours deployed in the defense of this nation to that most intense difficult peacetime assignment of recruiting young Marines into the Corps's ranks, a duty that he successfully completed twice, Colonel Studdard, accomplished his assigned missions and ensured that his Marines were professionally led and their needs met.

"The leadership traits and principles that he learned as a private at Marine Corps Recruit Depot Parris Island, reinforced at Officer Candidates School and The Basic School at Quantico, Virginia, and practiced throughout a stellar Marine Corps career now serve him well in his corporate experience at The Home Depot.

"Transition from active duty to the civilian work force is generally an action that we who have served our country faithfully are never really prepared for. Colonel Studdard's insights as to his own transition from the Marine Corps and, dare I say, personal transformation, can be a valuable lesson learned for all who must take off the uniform."

—Major General Charles Hudson, USMC (Ret),
Senior Associate at Booze Allen Hamilton

"I had the privilege to serve with Ted during part of his journey. He was a critical element in the most demanding, complex and high-risk training in the Marine Corps, and arguably close to the most demanding in the world. In addition to teaching, coaching, and mentoring artillery Marines and units in complex live-fire integration with aviation-delivered fires and ground maneuver, he played a vital role in safety backstop. This was crucial as pressure built, speed of decisions accelerated, the margin of error diminished, and the consequences of errors moved towards catastrophic. His measured voice over the radio managing Marines and units covering hundreds of square miles was a calming influence for our trainer-controllers and the exercise force. For me, as the responsible officer for both the safe execution and effectiveness of training, and steward for this most essential program to ensure readiness of marines to fight the nation's battles, Ted's presence was a rock upon which I was able to perform my duties. *Depot to Depot* captures those lessons from a US Marine who mastered those elements of leadership that have ensured Marine Corps success under the most demanding of circumstances for nearly 2 ½ centuries and presents them in a way that enable universal application to any environment."

—Major General Melvin Spiese, USMC (Ret), Chairman of
the Board of Directors at Active Resources, Inc

"*Depot to Depot* is more than an outstanding leadership book. It is a testimony to a life well lived that has been driven by honesty, integrity, humility, and hard work, which also happen to be the core traits of any effective leader."

—**B. J. Hebert**, President Occidental Chemical Corporation

"Colonel Studdard masterfully weaves leadership lessons learned in the Marines with compelling real-life stories of transformation, development, learning, trusting, collaborating and solving problems. His experiences will ring true to any business leader without military experience and clearly make the case for today's business organizations to seek out the talent coming from our military as they transition into the private sector. For those who have served, Colonel Studdard's transformation back to civilian life sets a bar for applying the leadership lessons of over 30 years of service in the Marines into today's dynamic and ever-changing business environment."

—**Dick Leinenkugel**, President and Chief Beer Merchant, Jacob Leinenkugel Brewing Company

"Ted Studdard captures the great lessons of leadership, tenacity, and culture that allow transitioning military leaders to make a real impact on corporate America!"

—**Dr. Wes Naylor**, CAPT, USN (RET), Founder and CEO, Fifty Pound Brains

"In sharing his own experiences throughout *Depot to Depot*, Ted Studdard delivers a book that makes leadership relatable and offers a clear message: leadership is an opportunity available to each of us and a responsibility to take seriously and with care."

—Jennifer Walsh, National War College, Class of 2007

"*Depot to Depot* does not just provide value to those looking to transition from the military to corporate America, it is a leadership experience that can benefit all who read it. Ted's ability to tie his personal experiences to his leadership journey and pass on lessons learned for leveraging and balancing experience, pride, and humility gives us a unique glimpse into the life of a great leader, and reminds all those searching for talent how invaluable of a resource our veterans truly are."

—David Pearson, Senior Director of Human Relations, The Home Depot

"Our military veterans return with a wealth of experience and knowledge few could ever encounter in a lifetime of corporate work. Their transformation presents companies with an opportunity to listen, learn and build a stronger generation of leaders, together. Successful transformations take patience and focus from both sides. *Depot to Depot* shows us how, whether you are a CEO hiring thousands of leaders or a veteran looking for your first job back in the States."

—Bob Pearson, Vice-Chairman of the Board, VETTED Foundation; Professor for U.S. State Department Marketing College; Strategic Advisor, W2O Group

"*Depot to Depot* is a must read for not only transitioning veterans but for those looking to hire veterans. Ted has done a great job in capturing many of the challenges veterans face as they make the difficult transition from the military to the civilian world. His personal journey provides teachable insights that can assist others that follow in his footsteps and offers employers a better understanding of the value of adding veteran leaders to your team."

—Beau Higgins, Senior Manager, Military Affairs Team
at Amazon

"Col. Studdard masterfully combines captivating tales from his military career with the practical advice required to navigate a return to civilian life. He unfolds a unique vision of linking leadership skills across career paths that is insightful to his fellow veterans and Corporate America."

—Tim Warren, President, United Community Bank

"Ted is an awesome example of leadership. His transition from the military to corporate life resonates with what I had to do as an NFL athlete. I would encourage everyone who's going through something tough to give this book a read and gain real steps to keep your feet moving. Thanks, Ted, for being authentic in your work!"

—Cory Procter, Pro Capital, LLC; NFL Alumnus

"Colonel Ted Studdard epitomizes the perspective that military veterans serve our country twice—first in uniform protecting our country, and subsequently as leaders in the business community. In *Depot to Depot,* Ted chronicles the lessons learned during his exemplary career as a Marine. With service in multiple overseas combat zones coupled with the challenging stateside assignments, Ted's experiences are rich with leadership insights on what it takes to succeed in both military and civilian organizations. Importantly, Ted exemplifies what it means to be a selfless leader, serving with both pride and humility. His book was a great read and it's a privilege to work with him at Home Depot, where the benefit of his leadership is now helping our managers be their very best."

—**Shane O'Kelly**, Senior Vice President, The Home Depot Pro

Depot to Depot:
A Transformational Leadership
Journey from the Military
to Corporate America

by Colonel Ted Studdard, USMC (Ret)

© Copyright 2019 Colonel Ted Studdard, USMC (Ret)

ISBN 978-1-63393-919-6

Published by

◤ köehlerbooks™

210 60th Street
Virginia Beach, VA 23451
800–435–4811
www.koehlerbooks.com

ALL OF THE AUTHOR'S PROCEEDS GO TO SUPPORT
VETERAN TRANSITION, MENTORSHIP AND
PROFESSIONAL MILITARY EDUCATION.

DEPT
TO
DEPOT

A Transformational Leadership
Journey from the Military
to Corporate America

COLONEL TED STUDDARD, USMC (RET)

VIRGINIA BEACH
CAPE CHARLES

DEDICATION

To Melissa, Alexis and Ward, with all my love.

And to the four Marines who inspired this journey:

      My dad, Sergeant William M. Studdard, Jr., USMC

      My uncle, Corporal Martin Melton, USMC

      My mentor, Sergeant Major Lyndolph Ward, USMC (Ret)

      My mentor, Colonel Richard E. Hawes, Jr. USMC (Ret)

CONTENTS

FORWARD

LIEUTENANT GENERAL RICHARD MILLS, USMC (RET),
President and Chief Executive Officer,
Marine Corps University Foundation

Colonel Ted Studdard's distinguished career in the United States Marine Corps was marked by assignments requiring strong, determined and compassionate leadership skills. Whether it was in staff or command billets, every assignment saw Ted successfully building and then leading teams of Marines as they flawlessly executed extremely demanding missions. His rise from Private to Colonel itself was remarkable, and each step up that ladder saw Ted given more and more responsibility and leaders placing higher and higher expectations on his results. As he rose in rank, he drew lessons and examples from the leaders he worked for and incorporated them into his own style and brand and exhibited the ability to modify and adapt his leadership style as situations changed. Yet some standards always remained constant. Take care of the Marines. Communicate to your troops. Accomplish the mission. He personified the Marine leader through his personal example, dedicated work ethic and ability to inspire loyalty and dedication in his people. Ted and his wife Melissa also taught those he led by the example they set that despite the challenges of military life, their love and respect for each other saw them through the separations and dangers of being a Marine.

Although I had heard of this talented rising officer before, I first had the opportunity to serve alongside Ted in Southwest Afghanistan in 2010. Ted was my Assistant Operations Officer running a Command Post that oversaw Marine and NATO units engaged in heavy combat with the Taliban 24 hours a day, for days at a time. To say it was demanding is a gross understatement. It was a brand new very diverse command team incorporating Officers and enlisted personnel from all the United States services, other governmental agencies, our NATO partners and from local Afghan military forces. It took strong leadership from Ted to first build an effective team in training and then lead the team as it made life and death decisions during the fighting. He exercised his remarkable leadership skills learned and developed over his challenging career to forge a remarkable effective team that contributed significantly to our success that year.

Although he has retired from the Corps, Colonel Studdard's days of contributing and mentoring people are not over. He has taken his unique experience and skill set learned in his 30-year career and applied them to the corporate world. Corporations expect their young managers to lead and inspire, and Colonel Studdard has clearly and concisely laid out how to do it. His distillation of lessons learned as a Marine provides a great guidebook for people leading teams whether at the work site or in corporate hallways.

Colonel Studdard also continues to "take care of the troops". The toughest part of a military career is often the transition period as folks take off the nation's cloth and don a suit and tie. Colonel Studdard's lessons learned as he made that very successful move in his life will be of significant value to service personnel as they begin that next chapter of their lives.

Colonel Studdard's service to Corps and Country inspired literally thousands of Marines whose lives he touched, and now he offers that same inspiration to the civilian world. I am sure that he'll soon be able to report "mission accomplished". Semper Fi.

PREFACE

I often speak with companies that are trying to incorporate veterans into their organizations, and with veterans who are looking for a second meaningful career that capitalizes on their vast experience. Across the country, I see a genuine desire to employ veterans, but there is often a gap in understanding the true value of the veteran. Conversely, there is a gap in the veteran community's understanding of how Corporate America works and how veterans can utilize their experience for a rewarding second career.

Our country's enduring success rests on a prosperous economy. The economy provides the foundation for our nation's security, our nation's growth and our global stability. Human capital is our nation's greatest asset, and the American people are our greatest resource. The return on the investment in human capital provides a strong economic foundation for our future. One of the untapped sources of human capital in America is our veteran community. My goal for this book is to help Corporate America understand its veterans and to leverage this enormous talent pool. Concurrently, I want to help our veterans understand the transformation they will experience and the opportunities for continued growth and contribution to our country via Corporate America.

When I set out to write, my plan was to illustrate the experiences and lessons learned that are common to our senior military leaders. I did not intend to write a leadership book; however, looking back at the lessons that great leaders taught me, leadership is a central theme and perhaps the most important part of this book.

A disclaimer: Many Marine and military titles as well as Home Depot terms that are typically capitalized internally have been lowercased in accordance with the grammatical standards of the Chicago Manual of Style. This style is not intended to dishonor either of these worthy institutions.

Thank you for joining me on this journey of leadership, transition and transformation.

TRANSITION is continuous. We are in a state of transition daily— physically, personally, and professionally.

TRANSFORMATION is a subset of transition; an intense period of change and growth.

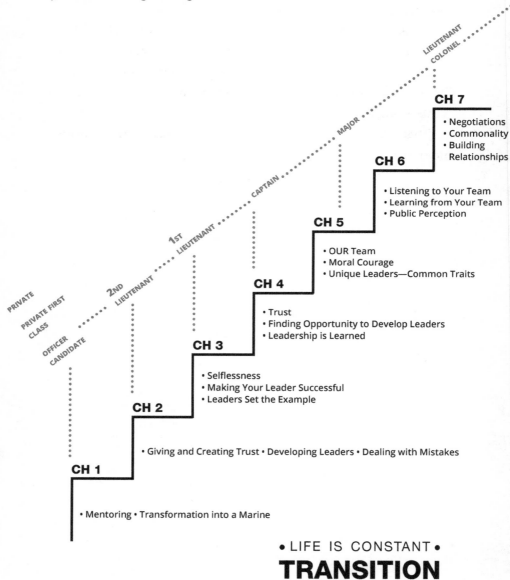

CH 7
- Negotiations
- Commonality
- Building Relationships

CH 6
- Listening to Your Team
- Learning from Your Team
- Public Perception

CH 5
- OUR Team
- Moral Courage
- Unique Leaders—Common Traits

CH 4
- Trust
- Finding Opportunity to Develop Leaders
- Leadership is Learned

CH 3
- Selflessness
- Making Your Leader Successful
- Leaders Set the Example

CH 2
- Giving and Creating Trust • Developing Leaders • Dealing with Mistakes

CH 1
- Mentoring • Transformation into a Marine

PRIVATE
PRIVATE FIRST CLASS
OFFICER CANDIDATE
2ND LIEUTENANT
1ST LIEUTENANT
CAPTAIN
MAJOR
LIEUTENANT COLONEL

• LIFE IS CONSTANT •
TRANSITION

TRANSFORMATION
Into A Marine

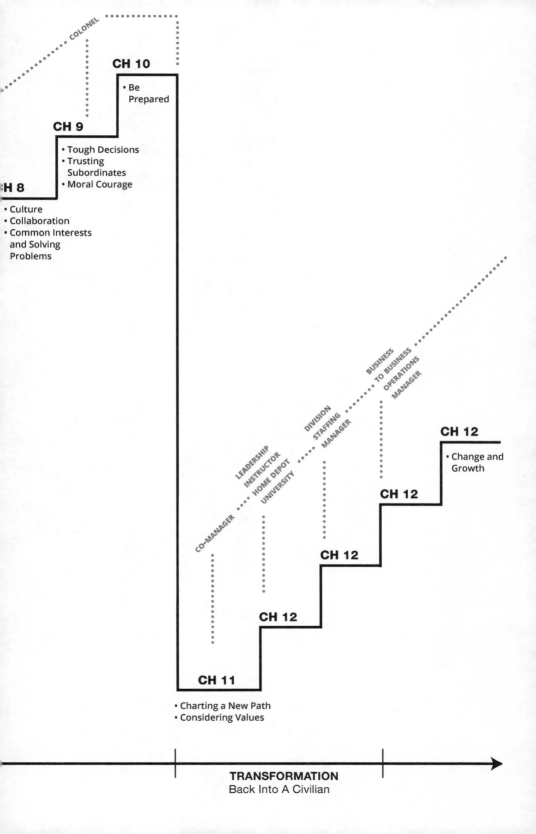

PROLOGUE

Just as I began to think this could still work out, the door burst open and the doctor rushed in, pushing Melissa aside, followed by several nurses, all of whom moved with a sense of urgency. My expression must have given me away; he answered my unasked question: "You are having a heart attack!"

In that split second, everything slowed down; I thought that there had to be a mistake. Some old guy was in another room having a heart attack and needed help and the medical team was in the wrong room—this could never happen to me. Didn't these people know that I was a Marine? Didn't they know that earlier in the week I completed my annual Combat Fitness Test with a perfect score? Didn't they know I had never missed a day of work?

Just like the verse from Baz Luhrmann's song "Everybody's Free (To Wear Sunscreen)," the events that change your life are the events that "blindside you at 4 p.m. on some idle Tuesday" when you least expect them and often when you are least prepared. This was definitely the case for me. An uneventful Saturday morning trip to the airport turned into a life-changing event. Transformative events happen to people every second around the world, and many of these experiences are unpreventable. Some, like mine, while not preventable, could have been mitigated with a bit of foresight and planning. The series of events that followed my Saturday morning episode opened my eyes to mistakes I had made in preparation—or better yet the lack of preparation—for my inevitable exit from the active duty ranks of the US Marine Corps.

I will provide a bit of background before we begin our journey from the Marine Corps Recruit Depot at Parris Island, South Carolina, to The Home Depot in Atlanta, Georgia.

I grew up in Commerce, Georgia, a small mill town of 3,000 where everyone knew everyone else. The boys I played football, basketball and baseball with in grade school were the same kids with whom I graduated from high school.

My parents, Bill and Rudene Studdard, were influential role models and were very involved in the community. They believed in manual labor and they took to heart that an idle mind is the devil's workshop. I always had a list of chores and projects to do, and each was inspected before it was deemed complete. I did not appreciate the life lessons or work ethic I was learning at the time. In addition to placing a strong value on hard work, my parents also encouraged me to pursue my passions. When the work was finished, I was on the field or the court, playing ball.

My dad was the local insurance agent, but prior to starting his business, he served a tour in the Marine Corps. My uncle, Martin Melton, was also a Marine; he served in World War II and fought in some of the Marine Corps' toughest and most iconic battles at Guadalcanal, Peleliu and New Britain. Although he never talked of battle, he occasionally shared stories about his time in the Corps.

After the war, his house burned, and he lost all of his Marine Corps memorabilia, including his medals. Nearly fifty years later when I was the commanding officer of Recruiting Station Nashville, my sergeant major, Ethbin Hayes, helped me work with the Veterans Administration to replace Uncle Martin's medals. When we received the medals, I invited Uncle Martin to be my guest at our annual Marine Corps Ball. Before the ball, our unit held an awards ceremony, and we invited him to join us. Unaware that the ceremony was in his honor, he joined at the appointed time and sat in the back of the room. I will never forget the surprise, the pride and the sense of humility he displayed when he was called forward. As I pinned the medals to his jacket, he whispered, "I'll get you for this, knucklehead." I will cherish that moment forever.

Growing up, I loved hearing the Marine stories and sensed the unspoken pride from both my dad and uncle; it was clear that the Marine Corps shaped their lives. They were my inspiration for joining the Marine Corps.

I decided to enlist in the Marine Corps early in my senior year of high school. My plan was to serve my initial four-year enlistment, then follow my father's footsteps into the insurance business.

(L-R:) Private Ted Studdard; my dad, Private Bill Studdard;
my uncle, Corporal Martin Melton.

CHAPTER 1

"Right is right and I don't give a damn if nobody is doing it; wrong is wrong and I don't give a damn if everybody is doing it."

—SERGEANT MAJOR LYNDOLPH WARD

THEMES: • Mentoring • Transformation into a Marine

I graduated from high school on a Saturday afternoon and departed for boot camp in the South Carolina Low Country before the sun rose Monday morning. Boot camp at Parris Island was noisy (Marine drill instructors have a way with words), hot, tiring, and exhilarating. I loved the training, and, even more, I loved being a Marine. Near the end I was selected for a meritorious promotion from private to private first class, which to this day is the promotion that means the most to me. It was the first time that I was away from home and truly on my own. Success or failure rested on my shoulders. The Marine Corps did not care who we were, where we came from, what we had or did not have; we were all on an equal footing, and we were measured on performance. Success was earned through teamwork, hard work, and commitment, which, thankfully, were lessons my coaches and parents taught me.

After a whirlwind thirteen weeks of training, I graduated boot camp at the end of summer and then departed for the University of Georgia in Athens where I majored in business management. I intended to complete my enlistment in the reserves while in college and then join my dad's insurance business. However, during my first week of school, I saw a Marine in uniform walking across the campus. There were no Marine bases near the university, so I did not expect to see this. I walked over and introduced myself.

"Good morning, sir. I am Private First Class Ted Studdard. May I help you?"

He was a Marine captain and the Marine Corps selection officer for Georgia. After a brief conversation, he asked me if I would like to become an officer and explained the process.

I would have to apply to the Platoon Leaders Course (PLC), designed for college students so they could attend Officers Candidates School (OCS) at Quantico, Virginia, during their summer vacations. The PLC program was divided into two parts, junior and senior. Prospective officers would have to successfully complete both parts of OCS during the summers, and they would be commissioned as Marine second lieutenants after graduation.

It was a quick and easy decision. An opportunity to go from private first class to second lieutenant was a no-brainer; I applied right away. It was a six-month application process, but finally I was accepted and discharged from my enlistment. I was on the path to becoming an officer.

The summer between my freshman and sophomore year, I went to the PLC junior session and then to PLC seniors between my junior and senior year. I must be a glutton for punishment because OCS was like boot camp for officers. It is a screening and weeding-out process that the Marine Corps uses to select potential officers. Both the junior and senior courses were six weeks long and designed to physically and mentally exhaust candidates to see how well they learned, worked together, led, and prioritized with limited time in a high-stress environment. Academics, physical fitness, leadership, and teamwork were graded daily by both instructors and peers. The majority of candidates starting as freshmen did not finish. Fortunately, I enjoyed this environment, and the experience from boot camp helped immeasurably. It was tough, but I loved the challenge. It also helped that my girlfriend, Melissa, and parents were very supportive.

A story about my close friend Bobby Cagle illustrates the level of commitment the candidates had to becoming Marine officers. Our final physical evaluation was a timed six-mile endurance run through a grueling obstacle-filled course up and down the wooded Quantico hills in combat gear including rifle and helmet. Bobby had broken his foot the previous week but knew he had to complete the final event to graduate OCS, one of the two requirements for becoming a Marine officer, the other being a college degree. He endured the pain through the week, and on the morning of the run, he laced his boots as tight as he could stand and attacked the course. Bobby not only completed the course, he outperformed nearly every other candidate on the event, earning the highest possible score. Bobby would go on to become a colonel serving for thirty years.

One of my classmates from Georgia, Doug Huseman, also went through the PLC program with me. After Doug and I graduated from PLC juniors, his dad, Dr. Richard Huseman, introduced us to Dick Hawes Jr., a retired Marine colonel who had recently moved to Athens. Colonel Hawes invited us to his office for a visit, and after a few minutes talking about our goal to be Marine officers, he said that he had someone he wanted us to meet and invited us to come back the following week.

At the appointed time, we arrived at his office where he introduced us to Sergeant Major Lyndolph Ward, a Marine who fought in World War II, Korea and Vietnam and earned nearly every Marine Corps combat award. He was an incredible figure—a tall, lean, hard-looking man. Here was a true living character like those John Wayne and Clint Eastwood portrayed in the movies. He had a certain swagger and was the essence of a Marine in the way he talked and presented himself. Furthermore, Sergeant Major Ward had a vocabulary of curse words that would make Webster envious. He filled every sentence with the most colorful phrases, delivered effortlessly, which left no room for misunderstanding.

Sergeant Major Lyndolph Ward, my early mentor.

The sergeant major and I soon developed a friendship that spanned two decades until he passed away. I am not sure what he saw in me or why he wanted to take me under his wing, but he did. We often met at Colonel Hawes' office, where I listened to these two heavily decorated leaders talk about life and the Marine Corps. It was a true incubator of leadership; they had seen, experienced and overcome some of the most difficult circumstances and leadership challenges imaginable. I did not realize at the time, but I was getting my first real experience with professional mentors. I was a sponge; Sergeant Major Ward spoke with me about leading young Marines, and Colonel Hawes talked about organizational leadership and being an officer. Both repeatedly emphasized the importance of moral courage—the willingness to do what was right regardless of circumstances. Sergeant Major Ward summed it up best by saying, "Right is right and I don't give a damn if nobody is doing it; wrong is wrong and I don't give a damn if everybody is doing it."

Sergeant Major Ward knew Melissa and I had a future together even before we did. As the time drew near for graduation and commissioning, he spent more and more time with me, often asking me to bring Melissa. I had no idea where I would go as a Marine, but I knew I wanted Melissa to be part of the journey.

Before leaving for my initial officer training at The Basic School in Quantico, Virginia, Sergeant Major Ward invited us to meet at his house. We sat at the kitchen table where he was smoking cigarettes and drinking coffee. The sergeant major started the conversation, "Ted, I'm talking with Melissa today." He put his cigarette down and looked Melissa in the eyes and asked, "Sweetheart, are you ready for this? Are you really ready for this? The Marine Corps is like an evil mistress. She is going to call and interrupt major life and family events. You will always compete with the mistress for Ted's attention. God forbid, she could even take him away to never return." Melissa's eyes grew as he continued. "When the drum rolls, he will leave; it doesn't matter if it's a holiday or if he just returned from somewhere else. He has a duty to his country and to the Corps."

Although we did not fully realize the wisdom and foreshadowing of his words at the time, the conversation opened our eyes to the level of commitment that would be required to follow this path.

CHAPTER 2

"Do you know where the mortars are?"

—CAPTAIN MARK SINGLETON

THEMES: • Giving and Creating Trust
• Developing Leaders • Dealing with Mistakes

Immediately following college graduation, Sergeant Major Ward and Colonel Hawes planned and officiated the ceremony commissioning me as a second lieutenant. During the ceremony, Colonel Hawes surprised me by giving me his Mameluke sword, the most cherished part of a Marine officer's uniform. When a senior Marine officer passes his sword to a young officer, it signifies trust. He was symbolically saying, "I believe in you, and I trust you to carry on the Marine Corps tradition." It is a bond and brotherhood with tremendous meaning. I used his sword for every ceremony and parade I participated in as a Marine, eventually passing it on to Sergeant Major Ward's grandson, Second Lieutenant Ward Ault, when he graduated from the US Naval Academy and was commissioned as a Marine second lieutenant.

Colonel Hawes watching my parents, Bill and Rudene Studdard, pin on my bars as a newly commissioned second lieutenant.

My first assignment was for six months at The Basic School (TBS) in Quantico, Virginia, where all newly commissioned Marine officers learn the basics of being an officer and an infantry platoon commander. Melissa stayed in Georgia working and preparing for our wedding.

Eight of my fellow lieutenants were in our wedding. On Friday night, as we ended our final week of field training, we cleaned and turned in our weapons, washed our field gear and then departed for Georgia. We drove all night from Quantico to Commerce, Georgia, arriving at 7 a.m. with plenty of time to spare for the 3 p.m. wedding. We slept a bit, scrubbed away the remaining dirt and camouflage paint and then did a quick rehearsal. Thankfully, my closest friend and college roommate, Brent Wood, who was also a Marine sergeant, was my best man. All young officers need the steady hand of a strong sergeant to get things right, and we were no different. Brent soon had us squared away and ensured we each knew what to do.

Melissa looked beautiful, and, thanks to Brent, the ceremony was perfectly executed. After the wedding, everyone gathered behind the church along the oak tree–lined sidewalk. The Marines marched into formation along either side and formed an arch with their swords. Melissa took my arm, and I led her down the sidewalk through the arch. As we passed through the last set of swords, my roommate, Second Lieutenant Paul Svitenko, swatted Melissa on the rear end with his sword and gave her the traditional "Welcome to the Marine Corps, Mrs. Studdard." Our Marine Corps life officially started.

It was all good fun for my friends and me, but it was a foreshadowing of the future for Melissa. She did everything for the wedding by herself, and I just showed up. This type of thing happened many more times throughout our lives. Melissa was a natural Marine wife; she understood my job, the associated duties and that I was a Marine twenty-four hours a day, seven days a week. She accepted what Sergeant Major Ward told her. Little did we know the magnitude of service and sacrifice she would make in the future.

We did not have a honeymoon, as I was due back to Quantico the Monday after our wedding. Melissa stayed in Georgia to pack our few belongings for our first move, which would be to Fort Sill in Lawton, Oklahoma, for artillery training before going to our initial Fleet Marine Force duty station, Kaneohe Bay, Hawaii.

All Marine artillerymen go to Fort Sill for training; we first learned in the classroom and then trained in the field, where we worked on artillery tactics and perfected shooting skills with the howitzers. Melissa and I enjoyed the time together. A quick five and a half months later our class graduated, and we were off to Hawaii.

After a year of training, I was finally ready to join my first Fleet Marine Force unit: Battery B, 1st Battalion, 12th Marine Regiment. The check-in process lasted about a week and included drawing personal field combat gear like helmets, flak jackets and canteens, and meeting the unit leaders. On the second day of my check-in, the battery commander asked if I wanted to participate in a helo-borne artillery raid that the unit was doing that night. I said yes without any hesitation and called Melissa to let her know I would be home the next morning. The plan was to fly from one island to another, conduct the live-fire practice raid and return before sunrise.

This was my first real Marine mission. Everything went smoothly until it was time to return. The weather unexpectedly turned, and the winds picked up so much that the last helicopter could not extract the three-man forward observer team, which included me. We spent three days alone on an uninhabited island in the middle of the Pacific Ocean before the weather permitted our extraction. The mistress had spoken.

I felt like a character from *Gilligan's Island*. A three-hour tour became a three-day event. It was a unique indoctrination for Melissa and perhaps the best way to get started as a Marine wife because scenarios like this occurred again.

I was deployed for two of the three years we were stationed in Hawaii. Although I was never in Hawaii for more than three months at a time, it was an exceptional personal and professional experience. All of the junior officers were close. We cooked out and surfed together on weekends, developing relationships that served Marines and families well. When we deployed (pre cell phones), one of the seasoned Marine wives served as an ombudsman, and our unit leadership communicated back through her to the families. Her communication job was made much easier as a result of the bonds we had formed.

Our first large-scale training exercise was on the Big Island of Hawaii. In addition to our regular allocation of ammunition, we were given a new type of ammunition to train with during the deployment. The training area was one of the few places in the world with a range that supported live-fire training with this type of ammunition. The entire unit was ready to fire it, but the conditions were never right. We had been carrying the ammunition for several weeks and were eager to shoot it.

Early one morning, our commanding officer, Captain Mark Singleton, went to our higher headquarters to get briefed on our next mission. While he was gone, I was in charge of firing. We were in one of the few firing positions in which we could shoot this ammunition. It had been raining nonstop, but the sun came out, the skies cleared, and visibility improved dramatically. I thought it was a great time to shoot the new ammunition; I did not want us to miss this training opportunity. So I made the decision to shoot it. The Marines executed the fire missions perfectly.

Just as the last rounds impacted, I saw Captain Singleton returning in his Humvee. I knew he would be happy that we successfully accomplished that part of our training. When he pulled in I asked, "Sir, did you see it? We shot it. The Marines did a great job."

He looked at me and said, "Say again."

I repeated my comment and noticed he was not as happy about it as I was. He asked me again, and I repeated my report.

He then said, "Ted, do you know where everyone is in the training area? There are about 2,000 Marines here. Do you know where they are all located?"

As he started naming units, I confirmed that I knew the location of each unit, until he got to the mortars.

"Do you know where the Mortars are?"

As soon as he said that, I felt that cold feeling go down my spine as I replied, "No."

He followed with, "They are about two kilometers in front of you, and you just shot over their heads."

I immediately knew I had endangered their lives. Due to its lethality, this ammunition was only cleared to fire over the heads of friendly forces under the most extreme circumstances, which most definitely did not include a training exercise. Captain Singleton could have relieved me on the spot, and my brief seven-week career in the Fleet Marine Force would have been over; I would be finished as a Marine. He paused and then asked me to walk with him so we could talk privately.

"Ted, do you realize the impact of what you did?" he asked and followed with a few questions to make sure I truly understood. I felt he was just drawing it out. I wanted him to get it over with, fire me and let it be done.

I respected him and felt terrible that I had let him down and even worse that I endangered fellow Marines. As he finished speaking with me, he looked me in the eyes and much to my surprise said, "Ted, I believe in you and I trust you. You are one of my best lieutenants; don't make the same stupid mistake again. Now get out there and lead your Marines and train them well."

Captain Mark Singleton and I at the Marine Corps Birthday Ball in Honolulu, Hawaii.

To this day, that lesson still hits home. What happened demonstrated negligence on my part, but he saved me; he put his neck on the line for me. He could have fired me, but instead he created the trust and respect I still have for him today. It also let all the Marines in our unit know that he would stand by us if we made a genuine mistake. We all knew we had a strong leader who would push us, and who had our backs as long as it was not illegal, immoral, or unethical. That incident made a huge imprint on me as a leader, causing me to pause and think about what type of leader I wanted to be—would I be one to use moments like this to teach and build?

We deployed to Okinawa, Japan, for a six-month rotation just as Saddam Hussein's Iraqi forces invaded Kuwait. We knew we were eventually going to fight, but as the build-up of forces began in Saudi Arabia, we left Okinawa for a three-month combat work-up at Mt. Fuji, Japan. We departed for the field early on Monday mornings, conducted live-fire combat training all week, and then hiked the ten miles back to the base camp late on Friday evenings. As soon as we arrived, we cleaned our weapons, then our equipment, and once everything was accounted for and secured, we took care of ourselves.

We were all young; most of the Marines in my platoon were eighteen to twenty-two years old. On Saturdays we were up at sunrise for inspections—every week the unit leaders checked different essential items to ensure we were ready to go at a moment's notice. After the inspections, we reviewed guidelines for the weekend: take care of each other, be smart, don't get arrested, and be back to the base on time Sunday evening. We had a standing rule that if anyone returned late, his liberty (off-base privilege) would be revoked for the remainder of our deployment at Mt. Fuji. After the liberty brief, everyone headed to Tokyo for the remainder of the weekend. We knew we were going to combat, and we had nothing to spend money on other than a good time. We worked hard during the week and played hard on Saturday night. Returning on Sunday, we started the routine all over again.

Midway through our time at Fuji, one of my enlisted leaders broke the rule by coming back late. Would I give him a free pass because he was one of my key leaders or hold him to the same standard as everyone else? Despite knowing that he would be upset with me, I held him accountable. I did not like it any more than he did, but it was the right thing to do. At the time, I did not fully appreciate the positive long-term impact it would have on my platoon. They knew I would be true to my word, and, regardless of role or title, everyone would be held accountable for their actions. The consistency and accountability ultimately led to the sustainability of our team over time. Conversely, the absence of consistency and accountability can cause a unit or a business to lose its cohesiveness.

Through the years, I have seen a pattern emerge. Most leaders have to deal with an initial negative incident or event, and how it is handled sets the tone. If the leader deals with the situation appropriately, it is like putting money in the bank; however, if the leader handles it poorly, it's like making a withdrawal with insufficient funds. The leader begins in a deficit and has to work doubly hard to earn back the trust and confidence of the team.

CHAPTER 3

*"Always take the hardest, nastiest, toughest job
that nobody wants. That's where you will grow."*

—COLONEL WAYNE ROLLINGS

THEMES: • Selflessness • Making Your Leader Successful
• Leaders Set the Example

Our time at Mt. Fuji passed quickly. We returned to Okinawa in mid-December to load our howitzers, crew-served machine guns, individual weapons, radios, vehicles, and maintenance equipment on ships bound for Saudi Arabia. Many of the Marines stationed on Okinawa were deployed from stateside bases for six-month rotations. Our battery was one of those rotational units. By this point, we had been deployed away from our home base at Kaneohe Bay, Hawaii, for five months, and we were about to embark on another extended deployment. After loading the ships, we had a couple of weeks before we were scheduled to fly, so our battalion commander, Lieutenant Colonel Mike Swords, graciously allowed us to bring our families, wives, or girlfriends to Okinawa.

It was a surreal time; we were in a holding pattern trying to be normal in an abnormal situation. All we could do was wait. We held a formation every morning to account for everyone, followed by physical training and then liberty. Numerous Marines got married as we waited for our departure date to arrive. It seemed like we attended a wedding every day. Melissa and I enjoyed our time to the fullest, as did everyone else. Soon, after an unforgettable Christmas party with my platoon, we said our goodbyes and left for Saudi Arabia.

The flight to our debarkation point in Saudi Arabia took nearly two days with extended refueling stops in Alaska and Belgium. Upon arrival, we quickly moved into a base camp near the port, set up large tents and dug dive pits around each for protection against SCUD missile attacks. Little did we know that several hours later, we would be using the dive pits. In the middle of the night, the alarms alerted us that the Iraqis had fired SCUD missiles. We did not know where they would land, but we knew that our staging area was a prime target. When the alarm sounded, the entire camp poured out of the tents and dove into the pits in anticipation of the incoming missiles. Fortunately, we were not hit.

Camp 15, Saudi Arabia; our staging area.
Note the dive pits around our tents.

When the cargo ships arrived at the port, we immediately off-loaded our equipment and prepared to move north into the Arabian Desert toward Kuwait. The further north we moved, the darker the sky became from the oil wells the Iraqi army set on fire. Regardless of the time of day or night, the sky was always dark from the smoke, often making it hard to see even half the length of a football field. The grime, oil and smoke embedded into our skin, and the smell of burning metal, rubber, diesel, and flesh was everywhere. Aside from using a bit of water occasionally to rinse off my armpits, feet and crotch, I did not shower for over sixty days. The inside of my olive green sleeping bag turned slick and black from the oil and smoke on my body, and the smell was so bad that I could not zip it up. We all lost weight because we did not have enough food to replace all the calories we were burning; we were constantly moving forward toward Kuwait and combat.

Desert hygiene.

Every day we continued to train and rehearse battle drills. This proved to be a lesson for me. Despite all of our preparation over the last year, which included extensive live-fire training deployments to the Big Island of Hawaii, Okinawa, Twentynine Palms in California, and Mt. Fuji, we worked on improving our skills daily. This is applicable to any endeavor because there is always something we can do better. Organizations often arbitrarily determine they have achieved success and fail to see the need to improve. As a result, they lose to competitors who refuse to rest on their laurels. Complacency kills in business just as it does on the battlefield.

Fires from the oil wells. The smoke was a constant companion.

Based on our mission requirements, we reorganized by combining the battery's two gun platoons into one large gun platoon comprised of six howitzer sections, medium and heavy machine-gun teams and tank-killer teams. I was selected to be the platoon commander, and Gunnery Sergeant Antonio Adversalo, better known as Gunny A, was chosen as the platoon sergeant. He had twenty years of field experience to my one. I am forever grateful that he was always willing and ready to teach me. One of the many lessons I learned from Gunny A was the importance of making your leader successful as a way of taking care of your people. He knew that by teaching me, he was taking care of all the Marines in the platoon. Executing my job well enabled everyone else to do theirs and improved our collective performance.

Leadership teams are most effective when they leverage their individual strengths. Gunny A was as hard and tough as any man I have ever known, and he leveraged that very well in his role. He took care of the daily routine, which gave me time to focus further out.

The lessons Gunny A taught through his example about trust and teamwork are still with me.

As the ground war unfolded, we were constantly shooting and moving. Our advance party moved ahead of the main body to select and prepare our next fighting position so the rest of our unit could occupy it quickly and quietly. This technique enabled us to move rapidly from position to position and to be ready to fire almost immediately.

We were aware the Iraqis emplaced unmarked minefields to impede our movement as they retreated across the desert. We were well into Kuwait and had been shooting and moving continuously for about thirty-six hours when our advance party was ordered to move again. Leading the small convoy, I was on the passenger side of the lead five-ton truck; Gunny A stood on the middle seat manning the .50 caliber machine gun mounted to the roof. Suddenly, the driver slammed on the brakes and anxiously said, "Sir, we are in a minefield." I looked down, and in the dim light I saw several mines partially buried in the sand.

Minefields have multiple purposes beyond destroying people, vehicles and equipment. Often the greater purpose of a minefield is to alter or stop a unit's movement in order to engage it with weapons that are more lethal. We had two options: we could try to back our vehicles out, or we could push forward.

We were in a bad position, and the longer we sat, the worse it would get. Quickly deciding our best option was to move forward through the minefield, I climbed out of the truck to lead the vehicles through. The tan land mines blended into the sand, the lack of visibility compounded by the smoke obscuring the little remaining sunlight added a degree of difficulty. Gunny A was on the ground beside me before I took my first step. I asked what he was doing and without waiting for a reply told him to get back in the truck.

"Sir, I am not letting you do this by yourself. We are doing it together." He refused to let me walk alone. He was right there putting his life on the line. He did not have to, and I did not ask, but that was

Gunny A—selfless. He walked in front of the right tire and I walked on the left as we led the team through.

After the war, he was awarded the Navy and Marine Corps Commendation Medal for valor resulting from his selfless action, but that is certainly not why he did it. My favorite Bible verse is John 15:13, "Greater love has no man than to lay down his life for his friend." Gunny A epitomized that verse. He led by example and personified the type of teamwork Captain Singleton developed and nurtured, beginning a year earlier back in the Pohakuloa Training Area of Hawaii. Battery B, 1st Battalion, 12th Marine Regiment was very special. We were close then and remain so today.

Gunnery Sergeant Adversalo and I in Kuwait wearing new, clean uniforms, getting ready to return to Saudi Arabia and then home.

All the services downsized after the war, including the Marine Corps. I thought the decision to stay in or get out would likely be made for me. Lieutenants had to go through augmentation, which was a Marine Corps–wide selection process to determine which officers would be allowed to stay on active duty; those not augmented had to get out. Annual augmentation rates vary based on personnel needs, which, during this drawdown period, were less than 10 percent. About thirty eligible lieutenants from our regiment were competing for augmentation. Colonel Wayne Rollings was our regimental commander. He was a renowned Marine who had earned the Navy Cross in Vietnam, held the world sit-up record, and would later retire as a major general.

Colonel Rollings was responsible for interviewing and subsequently ranking all the lieutenants for augmentation from his command of several thousand Marines. Despite the requirements for his time, our interview lasted forty-five minutes. Each regimental commander had to write a recommendation for each lieutenant competing for augmentation. Many leaders assign this type of work to someone on their staff, but not Colonel Rollings. He took this responsibility seriously, personally conducting every interview and writing the recommendations himself. He was an exceptional leader who was involved and wanted the best for his Marines and the Marine Corps.

The augmentation process took several months. As it was going on, I was given the opportunity to join the family insurance business. It was a great opportunity, and I was lucky to have it. I wrestled with my choices, knowing that we would have an easier life and make a better living if I got out of the Marine Corps. I leaned toward my original plan of serving one tour and then going into business.

As my tour was winding down, our unit went to the Big Island for what I thought would be my last field training as a Marine—a month-long live-fire training exercise. I had just learned that I was one of the lieutenants chosen for augmentation, but I decided to decline and return to Georgia.

About a week into our training, Colonel Rollings appeared at our firing position. I was surprised to see him. He spoke with all the Marines and then asked me if we could talk for a few minutes. He reached into his flak jacket, pulled out his chewing tobacco, put in a huge chew and talked with me for about two hours. He told me about his family and about being a father and husband in the Marine Corps. He shared his experiences and his path as a Marine officer.

He wanted to know why I was thinking of getting out of the Marine Corps. He was genuine, he was transparent, and he listened. He gave me options and described what a Marine career could look like. He didn't pressure me or try to sell me on the Marines; he just talked to me like a father speaks with his son. He told me I had a future as a Marine.

He said he wanted me to go to The Basic School as a tactics instructor to teach new Marine officers. I never expected such an opportunity. It was incredible to have one-on-one time with him and even more so to have his endorsement for such an important assignment. Before Colonel Rollings departed, I asked him if he had any advice. He looked me in the eye, chewed and spit in the dirt and said, "Ted, always take the hardest, nastiest, toughest job that nobody wants. That's where you will grow."

I stayed in the Marine Corps because of him. A senior leader making the effort to spend time with a subordinate creates an impact. Colonel Rollings set the example and taught me the importance of investing one-on-one time. Returning home, Melissa and I discussed our options and decided to move forward with another tour.

CHAPTER 4

"Let's get out of his way and let him do it."

—COLONEL JIM CONWAY

THEMES: • Trust • Finding Opportunity to Develop Leaders
• Leadership is Learned

I was assigned as a tactics instructor at The Basic School in Quantico, Virginia. Teaching is a great way to learn your craft in depth, and I was elated to have this opportunity. There were thirty-five tactics instructors who taught the classes and ran the field exercises, including extensive live-fire training, for the six-month course. Each instructor was required to pass a rigorous qualification process that included subject mastery and teaching techniques for every class we taught before being approved to teach. We were divided into four sections—offensive tactics, defensive tactics, weapons, and leadership. Regardless of the class or event, leadership was central to everything we did. I was part of the defense section, and our team of captains and first lieutenants was responsible for all the defensive curriculum. I was fortunate to teach under the tutelage of Major Mike Ettore, an accomplished combat leader and superb mentor.

Beyond the rigor of the program, Major Ettore was methodical in helping us to prepare and deliver complex ideas in an understandable manner, which has served me well in every job since. Each week he shared a leadership lesson based on his experience to ready us for future roles as unit commanders. I performed a job I truly loved, learning more than the students the whole time I was there.

Our commanding officer was Colonel Jim Conway, who later became the 34th commandant of the Marine Corps. He was a tremendous leader who gave us the latitude and trust to do our jobs. A humorous example is the afternoon Colonel Conway and other senior officers from our tactics department and I scouted a new area for a company defense exercise. We were deep in the Northern Virginia woodlands when we punctured our tire. I was driving, and since I was the junior officer, it was my responsibility to change the tire. As I retrieved the spare, two of the majors decided it was a good time to provide unsolicited advice on tire-changing techniques. Colonel Conway overheard the comments and quickly stepped in.

"Men, Ted knows how to change a tire. Let's get out of his way and let him do it." And with that, he took them on a short walk to get them out of the way.

He subtly demonstrated a basic leadership lesson, which is to teach your people, then step back and trust them to do their jobs. He also ran interference so I could focus on the job at hand—Leadership 101.

Colonel Jim Conway promoting me to captain.

Lieutenant General Charles Krulak congratulating Melissa and me after the promotion. Lieutenant Colonel John and Stephanie Bates are pictured on the left. Lieutenant Colonel Bates, whose lung was shot out in Vietnam, is a hero in the truest sense and another exceptional leader with tremendous humility.

Another leader influential to my growth was Lieutenant General Charles Krulak, who soon became the 31st commandant of the Marine Corps. Captains Bob Petit, Randy Newman and I ran the three-day war, the graduation exercise for the six-month course, which all new second lieutenants were required to complete. It was a non-stop seventy-two-plus hours of simulated combat that crossed thousands of acres. Typically, the war extended over the weekend, and Lieutenant General Krulak would come out to see what was going on. He arrived alone before sunrise regardless of the weather and always took the time to speak with us. My real takeaway was not from the details of our conversations but from the example he set. Here was the most senior leader on base with tremendous responsibilities, yet he was consistently present to interact with his junior leaders. He stayed connected at the grassroots level without interfering or being a distraction.

We could have easily run the war using walkie-talkies to communicate instructions to our fellow tactics instructors who were with the students. However, our chief tactics instructor, Major Joe Medina, who later became the commanding general of the 3rd Marine Division, had us execute the command and control of the war as if we were operations officers in combat. We established and ran a fully functioning tactical combat operations center in the field, writing combat orders, conducting tactical resupply as well as preparing and executing reconnaissance plans. He even had us brief the senior Marines on base prior to every war just like we would in a real combat operation. This required an extraordinary amount of extra work, but he knew it was a learning opportunity for us as instructors. We worked hard; he allowed us to make mistakes, and we learned. Major Medina went the extra mile to ensure that both the instructors and the students were receiving training.

Fifteen years into the future, five of the instructors who taught at The Basic School during this time were colonels serving together in key combat leadership roles in southern Afghanistan. The leaders at The Basic School laid the foundation for our success through their personal investment in our growth.

These lessons are also applicable in corporations. We were in an organization where the culture was to pay it forward in order to make future generations of leaders better. Leadership is learned. You may be born with leadership traits, but leadership is an evolutionary process, developed through formal and informal schooling, mentors, self-study, and experience. The best leaders provide ongoing opportunities for their subordinates to gain experience and grow.

Following my tour at The Basic School, I was selected to attend the Amphibious Warfare School in Quantico, Virginia. It was a yearlong program to prepare captains for company-level command and higher-level staff roles akin to a corporate-level regional-leadership team. The selected Marines came from every military specialty. We also had students from the Army, Navy, Air Force and Coast Guard, as well as students from many of our allied countries, including Great Britain, Saudi Arabia, Japan, Korea, Italy, Norway, and Thailand.

We studied leadership, operational planning and execution, and learned more about how the overall Marine Corps enterprise functioned, but the most important thing we did was to build relationships with peers and allies.

Melissa and I sponsored Captain Kao Chung-Wu, a Marine from Taiwan. Spending time with Captain Kao and his family taught me that we often have more in common than we realize, especially when we are willing to look. In addition to being Marines, Captain Kao and I loved eating barbeque and spending time outdoors, and our daughters, both named Alexis, were the same age. Through these commonalities we began building a friendship.

The longer I interacted with people from different cultures, the more I became aware of our similarities as a global community. One of the basic commonalities is family. Regardless of where we are in the world, we want to take care of our families and provide for our children. When we think about building relationships, finding commonality helps us to connect. Once connected, we can then build teams and accomplish great tasks because we are more apt to look beyond differences to find similarities on which we can build.

Captain Kao enjoyed a long and successful career, retiring as a colonel. We still stay in touch.

CHAPTER 5

"Ted, do you think I am an idiot?"

—MAJOR GENERAL JOHN ADMIRE

THEMES: • OUR Team • Moral Courage
• Unique Leaders—Common Traits

My follow-on assignment to 2nd Battalion, 11th Marine Regiment, 1st Marine Division sent us across the country to Camp Pendleton, California, located between Los Angeles and San Diego. This was an especially meaningful assignment since I would be joining the same division that my uncle, Martin Melton, fought with across the Pacific in World War II.

A typical artillery battalion has three firing batteries and a headquarters battery with 650 to 850 Marines and sailors based on its task organization. Newly assigned captains generally serve in one of four functional areas during their first year on the battalion staff— personnel and administration, intelligence, operations, or logistics. I was assigned as the battalion logistics officer leading the team that handled maintenance, supply, facilities, budget and the overall logistics planning required to keep the battalion operating in any environment. Although not a professionally trained logistician, I had to work with my team and learn the role. In corporate terms, this was a career-broadening experience that gave me an understanding of the logistical planning and support necessary to keep a large organization operational anywhere in the world.

Our unit had warfighting responsibilities in two very different global regions. Winning in these complex environments required extensive field training under a multitude of difficult conditions at different locations. Logistical support for our robust training became very challenging with budget cuts. We did not have the funds to purchase the parts required to safely operate all of our trucks, machine guns and howitzers, which impacted our readiness—a term used to describe how prepared a unit was to fulfill its assigned role in a global crisis.

I was one of several officers, including our battalion commander, Lieutenant Colonel Mike Marletto, who joined the command during the summer rotation. As we prepared for our first large-scale live-fire training exercise with the new personnel, Lieutenant Colonel Marletto asked me why we were unable to take all of our Marines and equipment to the field. I informed him that we needed sixty-five additional tires to operate all of the vehicles in the battalion safely, and we did not have the budget to buy them.

Lieutenant Colonel Mike Marletto and I outside battalion
headquarters in Camp Pendleton, California.

Lieutenant Colonel Marletto asked me to review our budget and
determine what was required to be 100 percent complete with our
maintenance. Over the next week, I spent every working hour diving
into our maintenance and budget, sharing my findings with Lieutenant
Colonel Marletto. He requested that I write a brief outlining the issue
for our regimental commander, Colonel Joe Weber.

I expected Lieutenant Colonel Marletto to use the brief as part
of a discussion with Colonel Weber; instead, he arranged a meeting
with Colonel Weber during which I presented the findings. After
our discussion, Colonel Weber requested that I add a couple of
additional points and update the brief for our division commander,
Major General John Admire. I assumed that at this high level Colonel
Weber would use the brief as he spoke with Major General Admire
and the division staff. Again, I was wrong; he had me present the brief.

Researching and preparing the brief was a great learning
experience; interacting with senior leaders and gaining insight into

their thought process was an even better lesson. Yet the best lesson of all was the example of confident leaders giving me an opportunity to grow professionally.

I briefed Major General Admire on our budget and maintenance issues. He graciously listened, and when I finished, he said, "Ted, do you think I'm an idiot? Son, I know and I am sorry. I worry about this every day. You must realize that as political leaders change, our budgets also change. We have to learn to work within our budget restraints, and when we do not have the money, we have to be creative. Now, go figure out how to train your Marines."

He did not give me a plan, or allow room for excuses. He just told me to solve it. As much as it was not what I wanted to hear, it was exactly what I needed to hear. This is a basic lesson for success in tough times. You have to think, work a little harder and be creative. Regardless of the circumstances, you have to accomplish your mission. The solution we arrived at in this instance was to be even more vigilant with our budget, collectively do maintenance to be more efficient, and little by little we improved. We also succeeded in securing additions to the budget.

Lieutenant Colonel Marletto had a unique way of vesting his subordinate leaders with ownership of the unit and its success. Soon after taking command, he brought the leaders together and outlined the battalion's mission essential tasks—major tasks the battalion had to accomplish in order to fulfill its combat mission. He asked what we needed to do to ensure that we accomplished our part of the mission. He then tasked us to assess our capabilities in each area and create a training plan that prepared the unit for its combat mission. Instead of telling us what to do, he gave us a say in the plan, and it ultimately became our plan rather than his.

He was fully aware of what we were doing and occasionally stepped in to provide course corrections based on his experience. He let us enjoy our successes and held us accountable for our mistakes. When a leader includes subordinates in determining the organization's direction, the team gains ownership and executes at a higher level. Lieutenant Colonel Marletto knew exactly where he wanted us to go, but he had the confidence to allow us to take the unit there, which in turn helped us to grow and develop into a tight-knit team.

After a year as the battalion logistics officer, I was assigned to command one of the battalion's three firing batteries—Battery F. Soon I faced an unusual problem. We were training in the Mojave Desert and returned to our base camp late at night. As we inventoried our equipment and prepared to secure it for the night, our communications sergeant stopped by to let me know he had accounted for the communications equipment. Some of the equipment was highly sensitive and could compromise our communication globally if it was lost.

Something did not seem right in his demeanor, so we rechecked and discovered that a piece of sensitive equipment was missing, and he had not reported it. As we dug deeper, we found that a Marine who had been in trouble with the sergeant hid it in the desert.

I immediately contacted Lieutenant Colonel Marletto, who in turn notified the next leader in the chain of command, Colonel Weber. Following protocol, a Marine Corps–wide message was prepared, alerting everyone about the possible compromise for which my unit was responsible. It was professionally embarrassing but vital for them to know immediately. The first inclination when something goes wrong is to angrily point fingers and assign blame versus solving the immediate problem. Having the courage to be patient and remain calm typically paints a clearer picture leading to a quicker resolution. Instead of being accusatory, Lieutenant Colonel Marletto gave me the time and space to resolve the problem. It took two days, but we found the equipment. Many leaders do not have the confidence or moral courage to stand by their subordinates in a crisis, but those who do earn the enduring loyalty, respect and trust of their subordinates.

Concluding my tour in Camp Pendleton, I was promoted to major, and we moved to Twentynine Palms, a Marine Corps base spanning over 900 miles in California's Mojave Desert. The base serves as the primary combat-training center for the Marine Corps. Many Marines and their families considered Twentynine Palms to be a hardship tour. It can be tough, living in the harsh, remote desert; however, I remembered Colonel Rollings' advice: "Take the hardest, nastiest, toughest job that nobody wants. That's where you will grow."

I was assigned to the Tactical Training and Exercise Control Group as the head of the artillery and indirect fires team. We were tasked with teaching, training and exercise control for all of the indirect fire and artillery units. This was the Marine Corps' most comprehensive live-fire combat-training exercise, a high-visibility event that lasted nearly a month. It was an enormous responsibility and another opportunity for professional growth. Our team was immersed in high-level combat training every day. Teaching tactics at The Basic School focused on small-unit, entry-level leaders. Now I was on the other end of the spectrum, working with seasoned leaders who led large combat units.

The members of our unit were nicknamed "Coyotes" and spent over 250 days annually in the desert learning firsthand the tactics and techniques that worked and those that did not work in this environment. We collaborated with the units, training them on these techniques to help them perfect their combat skills.

The Tactical Training and Exercise Control Group—The Coyotes in the Mojave Desert at Twentynine Palms, California.

The basic element we worked with was a regimental combat team consisting of ground, aviation, and logistical combat elements. A colonel led the team of several thousand Marines and sailors. It was a great opportunity to observe different leadership styles in a complex, fast-paced, high-stress context. Over my two years as a Coyote, several of the leaders stood out from the rest. I realized that despite their different personalities and unique leadership styles, they had several common characteristics.

First, each had a level of professionalism that was astounding. They knew their job, and they were professionally astute. They did not bring attention to themselves or try to tell people how good they were, they were always calm despite the chaos, and their demeanor spoke volumes.

Second, they communicated with clarity and brevity so everyone, from private to colonel, understood the purpose of the mission, why they were doing it and how their role tied in to the unit's overall success. They communicated to inform and to educate.

Third, they were aware of everything going on in their unit. Although several thousand Marines were scattered over hundreds of square miles of desert, they did not micromanage; they observed, listened and stepped in only when necessary. They trained their subordinates and empowered them to execute.

Lastly, they exhibited humility. They were experts in their profession, and everyone knew it, but they accepted responsibility for any unit shortcomings and held themselves accountable. They never treated themselves as special; they did what their Marines did. They slept on the ground in the cold, they trained in the rain, they were hungry and endured the same challenges as their Marines. In short, they elevated everyone, and their teams were very successful as a result, which showed in their morale and their superior level of performance.

The ultimate validation of these combat leaders was the success they had post-9/11. Two of these colonels reached the very top of the organization, becoming four-star generals—General Robert Neller, 37th commandant of the Marine Corps, and General John "Jay" Paxton, 33rd assistant commandant of the Marine Corps.

On a typical day, several thousand Marines moved across the desert in tanks, amphibious assault vehicles, helicopters, and on foot conducting live-fire attacks and defensive maneuvers on a simulated enemy. It was as close as you can get to combat, stateside. All the firepower was synchronized with movement on the ground and in the air. It was controlled chaos at best; often a split second or few feet was the difference between life and death.

We conducted a very detailed debrief at the end of every phase of the exercise. The intent was to be brutally honest, highlighting areas that needed improvement while providing recommendations on how to improve. Our role was to help educate and to help solve problems in an effort to improve combat effectiveness.

Majors made up the majority of our team, providing critiques, advice and recommendations to unit leaders who outranked us. It was a great lesson in moral courage. It would have been easy to tell the senior leaders that their units were great, but it would have been counterproductive over time for them, their units and the Marine Corps. Telling a high-ranking officer that his team is not measuring up and that they are part of the problem does not always go over well, but good leaders respect the feedback and appreciate the frankness.

The last artillery unit I worked with was led by my early mentor, Lieutenant Colonel Mark Singleton. The unit experienced growing pains, and I had to recommend corrections. I gave him the feedback along with possible solutions. We had a conversation that was a bit uncomfortable for both of us. He took what I said into account, his unit made adjustments, and ultimately they performed extremely well. Being willing to listen and accept tough feedback is challenging, but the ability to do so sets the best leaders apart from the others.

I learned that it is easy to pat people on the back, but effectively delivering constructive feedback without crushing someone's spirit or coming across as a know-it-all is a challenging yet necessary skill set.

Midway through our tour, the 7.1-magnitude Hector Mine earthquake hit the base. I was home for the evening, and we had gone out to dinner. On the ride home, our newborn son, Ward, fell asleep, so Melissa left him in the carrier and took him to our bedroom. Just before 2 a.m., Ward woke up and Melissa brought him into bed with us. Just as she got back in bed, our house began shaking violently with furniture toppling over and glass breaking throughout. Our old TV fell off the dresser, crushing Ward's carrier. The quake lasted for what seemed like minutes. Glass covered the floor, and it was dangerous to stay in the house, so I carried Melissa, Alexis and Ward to our vehicle in the driveway. All the Marines in our neighborhood were doing the same thing. Regardless of the earthquake, we had our job to do. As the aftershocks began, I made sure Melissa had food, formula, and diapers, kissed her goodbye and was on my way.

This is what Sergeant Major Ward meant years before. When the drum rolls and duty calls, you go. We left our families to ride out the aftershocks in our respective driveways as we headed back into the desert. This was life as a Marine family.

CHAPTER 6

"You are exactly where you need to be."

—MAJOR GENERAL JERRY HUMBLE

THEMES: • Listening to Your Team • Learning from Your Team
• Public Perception

I was selected to attend the Marine Corps Command and Staff College in Quantico, Virginia, during my second year as a Coyote. This gave me another year to study my profession with peers from across the US military, US government agencies, as well as allied officers. We also had an opportunity to sponsor Shaheen Ajlan, a Bharani naval officer, and his family. Our children went to the same school, and over the year our families spent quite a bit of time together. In addition to enjoying our friendship, Shaheen's insight on America politically, militarily and economically from an allied Islamic perspective was a priceless education.

**Melissa and I with Lieutenant Colonel Shaheen and Mina Ajlan at the
Marine Corps Command and Staff College
in Quantico, Virginia.**

Two weeks into the academic year, the Marine Corps held its selection board for recruiting station commanders. Approximately fifteen majors are selected annually to command one of the forty-eight recruiting stations across the country. This is the only command opportunity for majors, and it is a three-year command versus the standard two-year command due to the complexity of the role. From a corporate standpoint, this is both a career-broadening and stretch assignment. Typically, without prior recruiting experience, these majors are charged with leading a large, dispersed organization often several states away from the higher headquarters. The new commanders learn in great detail how the staffing and entry-level training process works, valuable knowledge for leaders in any organization. Everyone wanted to be considered, but most did not want to be selected; no one joins the Marines to recruit!

I was chosen to command Recruiting Station Nashville and charged with leading a team of Marines and civilians responsible for all Marine Corps officer and enlisted recruiting in Tennessee, North

Alabama and North Mississippi; 650 Marines, future Marines and civilians at thirty-two sites fell under my command. I was an artilleryman, and now I was in charge of a large recruiting command without any prior recruiting experience. Failure on my part would have a negative and very visible impact on the overall staffing for the Marine Corps. The duty is challenging, and the team is under a microscope. There were two equally important requirements for success: representing the Marine Corps in a positive manner, and recruiting for quality and quantity while following strict ethical guidelines.

Two months into command and still learning my role, I was walking out of our headquarters on my way to East Tennessee when my secretary, Glenda Weiler, frantically called me back inside. She immediately directed me to our conference room, where the television showed the ongoing attacks. I was shocked and angry as I watched the unimaginable become reality. It was 11 September, and we were inevitably going to war; like every other Marine, I was ready for the call. Two weeks after the attack, our commanding general, Major General Jerry Humble, flew in for a previously scheduled visit. He was a seasoned leader with both combat and recruiting experience. I just knew he would be giving me orders to report to an artillery unit to begin preparing for combat.

As the day unfolded, he did not mention the orders, so I let him know that I was ready to go to any unit preparing to deploy and that I would would resume command of the recruiting station once hostilities were over. I added that Melissa and I already discussed family logistics, and she and the kids would remain in Nashville for the duration of the deployment. I thought it was a great plan—use all of my artillery experience for something better than recruiting.

After listening, he looked at me and said, "Ted, you are exactly where you need to be, where the Marine Corps needs you, and you are going to stay and do this." I was dejected knowing that I would not be joining the fight and that the case was closed with no further discussion.

I was going to be on recruiting duty for the next three years, and, in order to be successful, I knew that I had a lot to learn. Leaders are normally among the most experienced and knowledgeable people on the team, but as I began my new role I was the least experienced and least knowledgeable. Thankfully, I had a solid core of stellar leaders like Chief Warrant Officer-2 Ron Harrell, Sergeant Major Ethbin Hayes, Gunnery Sergeant Scott Johnston, Staff Sergeant Neil George and many others who were willing to teach me the intricacies of recruiting.

Me with Sergeant Major Ethbin Hayes at the Marine Corps Ball in Nashville, Tennessee.

Unable to be everywhere at once, I had to ensure that everyone was trained and that they all understood our mission and what their role was in accomplishing that mission. Equally importantly, our command team and our training teams had to speak with one voice. We had to deliver the same message in an understandable manner repeatedly until it was ingrained. Synchronization was vital; we did not want to counter each other or confuse the message.

Our recruiting station achieved a major milestone during my first year of command. We accomplished our annual recruiting mission for twelve consecutive months, a first for Recruiting Station Nashville. Our team worked harder and put in longer hours than any other team I had ever been a part of, but I knew we could not continue at this pace. I realized I was driving the team to achieve my assigned metrics and mission when I should have focused on helping them to achieve their individual missions.

As we developed our annual plan for my second year in command, we decided to concentrate on the subordinate teams to ensure each team and its individual Marines achieved their respective missions. I borrowed from Lieutenant Colonel Marletto and let the team leaders set their respective part of the overall mission. I knew I was gambling on my career if it failed, but I believed that if we could make the Marines successful at the individual and small-unit level across the command, then our higher-level mission would naturally follow.

It worked. We became the top recruiting station, recruiting more per capita than any other command in the country. Most importantly, the Marines excelled individually, which helped many get promoted to the next level. The results are incredible when the team has ownership and their success is the focus.

We were enjoying our success when I learned a lesson on the power of perception. The staff, team leaders and I were completing our annual planning, and I wanted to treat everyone to a beer at a local sports bar near our headquarters. Just as all the beer arrived at our table, one of the local television reporters showed up with her camera crew. She had provided great support for us previously with several very positive stories that helped our recruiting efforts. She was there to get fan reactions to the Tennessee Titans, who were playing that night. When she saw our team, she asked if she could get some footage, and I said yes. What seemed like good public relations did not turn out so well. The next day I was at an event in Nashville when one of the leaders in the community mentioned seeing us all on television with a table full of beer bottles and subtly noted this might not be the best image for us to portray. All publicity is not good publicity, and perception quickly becomes reality. I put my team in a bad position, and I should have known better. Thankfully, we did not suffer any lasting repercussions, but the lesson stuck.

The Marines who served on recruiting duty were selected based on their previous successes and their future potential, yet some struggled. As the leader, I had to decide whether to retain them on this special duty or return them to their former unit, which would effectively end their careers. Business leaders face similar decisions. When making these life-changing decisions I found that it helped to consider the following:

1. Does the person have the capability for this role mentally, physically, and emotionally? If the answer is no, then the leader should help them find a more suitable role in the organization. If the answer is yes, then go to two.

2. Is the person trained for the role? This is a leader's responsibility. If the answer is no, then train them and review your internal training programing. If the answer is yes, then go to three.

3. Does the person have the drive and desire to be successful? If the answer is yes, then help. Often something going on outside of work is the reason for their poor performance. If the answer is no, remove them and give the opportunity to someone else.

I am convinced that people do not come to work to fail. Investing a little extra personal time and effort often makes a huge impact. Saving an associate or teammate provides a strong return on investment in time, in sparing the costs of recruiting and training replacements, in maintaining higher capacity, and in building loyalty and trust within the organization. The majority of performance-based issues that I have experienced have been a result of something negative going on in someone's life beyond work, and when it is resolved, performance typically improves.

This tour that I dreaded turned out to be extremely rewarding and helped me grow. I served with a team of hardworking, smart and dedicated Marines who taught me far more than I ever taught them. Once again, Colonel Rollings was right.

CHAPTER 7

". . . as we danced . . ."

THEMES: • Negotiations • Commonality • Building Relationships

As I finished year two of my three-year tour in Nashville, I received wonderful news. I was selected for promotion to lieutenant colonel. A few months later I received even better news. I was chosen to command an artillery battalion—3rd Battalion, 12th Marines, 3rd Marine Division—which would take me back to the operating forces. Headquartered in Okinawa, Japan, the unit was the Marine Corps' only artillery battalion permanently stationed outside of the United States.

Our unit's primary responsibilities centered on the Western Pacific, including North and South Korea. The region has long been on the edge of volatility given the global relationship with North Korea. Our location and our role in the defense of the Korean Peninsula combined with the combat missions of the teams we had in Iraq and Afghanistan mandated that we maintain a high state of combat readiness.

Okinawa is a small island in the East China Sea situated about 1,000 miles south of Tokyo. It is nearly seventy miles long with an average width of seven miles. Firing artillery and machine guns on Okinawa was problematic due to its size, population density and local politics. To help mitigate this problem, the United States entered into a series of treaties with the Japanese government that enabled our battalion to conduct four, one month-long, training exercises annually at various locations on the main Japanese islands. While the treaties provided the general parameters, each training evolution required its own series of negotiations both at national and local levels. These were extremely nuanced negotiations covering every imaginable detail from the daily time windows for firing all the way down to how we would catch leftover shell casings during our small-arms training.

We unknowingly created a bad precedent that, over time, began to inhibit our training. Every time a new commander rotated in and took over the negotiations, the US provided a relatively small concession as a demonstration of goodwill and expected the same in return, which never happened. While the individual concessions were not significant in and of themselves, when combined over time they limited the scope of our training. Our counterparts were either elected officials or political appointees with staffs comprised of longtime bureaucrats, many of whom had participated in these negotiations for years. They had a successful long-term strategic approach. On our side, the American team changed personnel frequently and did not have the same depth of corporate knowledge or long-range approach compared to the Japanese. Realizing how much we had lost over time, I decided to take a hard-line approach to our negotiations but did not make any headway. The harder I pushed, the more difficult the negotiations became.

Meeting with Japanese political leaders.

During each training deployment, my interpreter and I traveled with our Japanese counterparts to meet with local elected officials in the cities and towns near our training venue. After the meetings, we participated in press conferences and conducted interviews with the local, national and international media. Tremendous preparation went into these media events since a slip of the tongue or an unintentional gesture could create ill will or even lead to international issues. Initially, I was so focused on the events that I did not appreciate the position my counterparts were in and how they needed to be perceived to be reelected or to retain their position. Becoming more comfortable with the process and subsequently more observant, I realized they walked a political tightrope; they would never help us unless I had a better understanding of their needs and could help them achieve some of their goals.

The breakthrough we needed for our negotiations came unexpectedly. Prior to each of the exercises and in conjunction with the meetings and media events, the government of Japan would host a cultural dinner with local officials, national officials and the senior members of my battalion staff and occasionally they would also host a post exercise dinner. We had just completed a month of training in the most remote area that we used. The people who lived there were primarily farmers, and they invited our entire battalion along with the Japanese officials to a traditional BBQ at their outdoor community livestock arena.

The evening began with very little interaction; it was similar to a school dance with all the boys on one side and all the girls on the other, except in this case the Marines were on one side and the townspeople on the other. Soon the food was served, and everyone slowly began to sit in mixed groups at large picnic tables to eat. After dinner, there were traditional sake toasts and then a traditional dance. We all watched and laughed as our hosts began grabbing Marines and taking them into the center of the arena to join the dance. This was all good fun until a group of elderly ladies looped a scarf around my head and pulled me into the dance.

This was way out of my comfort zone, but I had no choice other than to participate. As we danced and circled around the arena, I noticed smiles and people beginning to communicate, some trying to use pocket language guides, others with hand gestures and many by sharing pictures. I saw my leadership team doing the same with our counterparts. The communication gap had been breached—no interpreters needed.

In the following months, our negotiations became less contentious, and we began to make progress. The social interaction helped us to focus on commonalities rather than differences, and relationships began to grow. Building these relationships enabled us to communicate more effectively, which helped us find solutions that achieved collective goals.

Several of the gracious hosts who helped find
commonality through a dance in Hokkaido, Japan.

Internal communication was vital for our battalion. In Nashville, I had Marines stationed in several states. Now I had Marines and sailors in multiple countries across the Asian continent, all conducting different missions simultaneously. The complexity of this distributed environment meant that decisions were often time sensitive, and delays could compromise opportunities or cause harm. To enable effective operations in this environment, I had to ensure that I clearly communicated our mission—what we were doing; my intent—why we were doing it; and the end state—the result we needed to achieve. Communicating the end state was the key. If my subordinate leaders understood the end state, they could make sound, timely decisions on the spot and alter plans to achieve the necessary results. Executing a plan perfectly is irrelevant if it fails to accomplish the mission.

Clear communication is equally important in the daily routine. We had a robust training program, which was directly linked to our mission essential tasks, and I assumed everyone understood why until one of my junior officers came back from Iraq. He had deployed to fill an individual role, and when he returned, he thanked me, saying he did not understand why the training was so exacting until he was in a situation where it helped him save lives. His comments validated the training; however, I realized that I had not done a good job of explaining the why behind our training.

I received my follow-on assignment during my second year of command. We were moving to Washington DC in the coming summer where I would become a student at the National War College.

CHAPTER 8

Who else had interests that intersected ours?

THEMES: • Culture • Collaboration
• Common Interests and Solving Problems

The National War College is the preeminent formal professional school for the United States military. The annual student body is comprised of a select group of colonels and lieutenant colonels from each branch of the military, as well as allied officers and key civilian leaders from major government agencies, including the Departments of Defense, Justice, and State, and the intelligence community. The class is evenly distributed among the three groups.

My year as a student at the National War College was extremely rewarding. A special aspect of the year was sponsoring a Hungarian army colonel, Zsolt Sandor, and his family. Early in his army career, Hungary was part of the Communist Eastern Bloc allied with the Soviet Union. Talking with Zsolt was fascinating. We often discussed being Cold War enemies and how our early careers focused on defeating each other. Now, less than two decades later, we were classmates enjoying family dinners together. The Sandors shared the holidays with us, including Christmas, which we spent with Melissa's parents on their cattle farm in Georgia.

Melissa and I with Katrina and Zsolt Sandor enjoying the afternoon on the our deck in Arlington, Virginia.

This was our third experience sponsoring an international officer and family. We were enriched with lifelong friends while also learning about different cultures, beliefs and worldviews.

The connections we made during these schools proved relevant in operations around the world. For example, when I was in command of 3rd Battalion, 12th Marines, our unit was part of Operation Unified Assistance, a humanitarian relief operation in response to the Indian Ocean tsunami that hit Indonesia and Thailand. Early in the operation, I flew across Sumatra with the Singapore military. As I boarded their helicopter, I was pleasantly surprised to meet the pilot, who was one of my Amphibious Warfare School classmates. A few days later, I went to a coordination meeting at the Australian Army's field headquarters and ended up working with an Australian classmate from the Command and Staff College. Subsequently, both in the Pentagon and in Afghanistan, I served with many of my National War College classmates. The challenges we faced were simplified tremendously because we had an existing relationship and a common foundation.

Being immersed in an eclectic group of people, all of whom were at the top of their professional game, made this an extraordinary year. A highlight was attending the French Centre des Hautes Etudes Militaires Colloquium in Paris with a small group of War College students selected to participate in the annual symposium between the two countries. The topic was culture and its role in conflict. Conducting this focused study into the impact of culture reinforced its importance in every aspect of our daily lives, from our local community to our global community. This experience further convinced me that taking the time to learn and understand culture is vital when trying to solve complex issues.

Sitting at Napoleon's desk in Paris, France.

The Sub-Saharan Africa team in Zambia.

I also traveled to Botswana and Zambia during the year as part of a team studying Sub-Saharan Africa. Our preparation included meetings with leaders from the African Union and ambassadors and diplomats from multiple African countries and the United Nations. These meetings, combined with our work and travel in Southern Africa, reiterated the significance and impact of culture on a global scale. Culture is equally important in business, whether creating a positive culture, changing a toxic culture or integrating a new team into the larger enterprise. If the culture—i.e., the foundation—is sound at the beginning, everything built on it will stand.

I was screened and selected midway through the school year to serve on the Joint Staff, based in the Pentagon in Washington DC. The role of the Joint Staff is to assist the chairman of the Joint Chiefs of Staff (CJCS) with unified strategic direction, unified operations and integration of the combatant commands. This includes developing policy, preparing and coordinating global strategic plans and overseeing their execution. The CJCS is the nation's senior military leader; his two primary duties are to serve as the senior military advisor to the president and to chair the Joint Chiefs, comprised of the service chiefs from each branch of the United States military. The Joint Staff has eight major directorates:

J-1: Directorate for Manpower and Personnel
J-2: Directorate for Intelligence
J-3: Directorate for Operations
J-4: Directorate for Logistics
J-5: Directorate for Strategic Plans and Policies
J-6: Directorate for Command, Control, Communications and
    Computer Systems
J-7: Directorate for Operational Plans and Force Deployment
J-8: Directorate for Force Structure, Resources and
    Assessments

The *J* represents the Joint Staff, and the number represents the staff function. This alphanumeric naming convention is standard for the US military and common globally.

Our operations team on the steps of the Pentagon, Washington, DC.

I served in the J-3, current operations, which focuses on strategic planning and execution from the present out to five years. I was on the team responsible for the Middle East and parts of Central and Southern Asia. This larger team was subdivided into three specialized teams—one for Iraq, one for Afghanistan and Pakistan, and one for terrorism and piracy around the Horn of Africa and the Arabian Peninsula.

The team was involved in every aspect of the wars in Iraq, Afghanistan and the overarching Global War on Terrorism, leading near-term strategic planning in close collaboration with US and allied governments and military partners. Several months into the assignment, I was assigned to lead the Afghanistan and Pakistan team. Once again, I was in a new environment and was expected to learn and contribute quickly. I could dedicate an entire book to lessons learned on the Joint Staff, from leadership to project management and strategic planning; however, I will limit it to a brief synopsis of two topics germane to business—collaboration and finding common interests to solve complex problems.

I didn't expect to see the level of collaboration that I did while serving on the Joint Staff. The magnitude of the decisions made or influenced by the Joint Staff required a process to create sound solutions and to facilitate timely decisions. The vehicle for this collaborative process was the operational planning team (OPT), a temporary team established to fulfill a specific purpose. Typically, the OPT was either given a problem to solve or a general end state to achieve, and its role was to create options for solutions. Once an option was selected, the OPT developed and published the strategic plans and oversaw global execution. The core of the OPT came from service headquarters, combatant commands and selected government agencies or departments and was led by a member of our team. Incorporating all the major stakeholders was crucial because it provided multiple ideas while creating buy-in. Everyone had a say and understood the thought process that informed the recommended solutions.

Three components of the OPT made it an efficient and effective process. First, it was standardized yet not rigid. The entire staff understood the flow of the OPT, the general steps that it would follow and how its output would be vetted and approved. The team did not have to define or debate the process since it was predetermined, which enhanced efficiency. Having a common understanding also allowed flexibility for the OPT leader, who, based on the situational requirements, could call an audible. No two OPTs were exactly alike; however, they did follow the same general sequence.

The second key to success was the convening authority, who had overall responsibility for establishing the OPT. The convening authority (a senior officer akin to a corporate senior vice president or executive vice president) opened the OPT with an overview of its purpose and mission, which included context beginning at the strategic level. As the OPT worked through the problem set, the OPT leader brought in the convening authority at predetermined points for updates, guidance or to make in-stride decisions to keep the process moving. The involvement at critical junctures prevented surprises and lengthy revisions.

The third component was the individual member. Each participating command or agency had a representative who was empowered to speak and make decisions for the organization within the context of the OPT. The members kept their leadership informed as solutions were being developed. This prevented the organization from being assigned a task it could not accomplish, which would have generated revisions and caused delays. It also facilitated concurrent planning and preparation. Since the subordinate commands were aware of the upcoming mission, they could begin their own internal planning and preparation while the OPT was still working.

Leading multiple OPTs taught me the value of having a common baseline process. It also taught me that having the convening authority involved at the beginning to provide overall direction and context along with built-in checkpoints enhanced communication and allowed for in-stride adjustments versus waiting to make major revisions at the end. Finally, I learned that the OPT process created better options than one person could working alone, and the options were viable for all of the organizations. Incorporating input from each organization created understanding, buy-in and a much more effective range of solutions.

I learned a valuable lesson about finding common interests to solve complex problems from the CJCS, Admiral Mike Mullen, early on a Saturday morning in the briefing room of the Pentagon's National Military Command Center. I was tasked to prepare an in-depth analysis for a potential threat and to lead a discussion on strategic options. Given a one-week timeline, I immediately assembled an OPT and we began work. The plan was to present the analysis and accompanying options to the chairman, vice chairman, director of the Joint Staff and the eight functional directors, followed by a discussion regarding the way forward.

A strong leader in challenging times, Chairman of the
Joint Chiefs of Staff Admiral Mike Mullen.

I opened the brief on the following Saturday morning at 8 a.m. to a packed room. The chairman, Admiral Mullen, US Navy; the vice chairman, General James Cartwright, US Marine Corps; and the director of the Joint Staff, Lieutenant General Stanley McChrystal, US Army, sat at the head table flanked on both sides by the eight directors, the J-1 through J-4 on the left and the J-5 through J-8 on the right. Standing behind them were senior leaders from each of the services. The first question came minutes into the brief and was very specific regarding a potential problem and associated options. The quiet shuffling of papers stopped, and the room became silent. As I paused to consider my response, Admiral Mullen interjected and redirected the conversation from a regional, military-centric conversation to a global conversation on relationships and common interests. The entire room had overlooked the most basic question— who else had interests that intersected ours concerning this potential problem, and what were our corresponding relationships?

Over the next three hours, we held a global discussion centered on national interests, current relationships, and improving or creating both personal and organizational relationships where they were lacking. It was a lesson about finding common interests and building relationships. The best leaders distill complexity into simplicity just as Admiral Mullen did on that Saturday morning.

Serving on the Joint Staff during this historically significant period was one of the high points of my career. While often mentally grueling with its own unique set of pressures, it proved to be invaluable for professional growth. As noted, I could write an entire book on the lessons I learned about leadership and character while serving in the Pentagon. These short stories only provide a glimpse and cannot do justice to the incredible leaders with whom I was privileged to serve. Once again, Colonel Rollings' advice to take the hardest, nastiest, toughest job that nobody wants was right on target.

Completing my tour on the Joint Staff, I received orders to the 1st Marine Division in Camp Pendleton, California. I was excited to rejoin the division; it meant I would be deploying to Afghanistan. Having spent the previous two years totally immersed in Afghanistan, I was eager to be a part of the Marine Corps expeditionary force that would be executing a new and essential part of our nation's Afghanistan strategy.

CHAPTER 9

"What do you want to do?"

—COLONEL PAUL KENNEDY

THEMES: • Tough Decisions
• Trusting Subordinates • Moral Courage

As the last day of the school year ended for Alexis and Ward, we departed Washington DC and began our drive across the country to California. The week we arrived at Camp Pendleton, I learned I was selected for a command assignment. Command selection takes precedence over every other assignment and is usually done a year in advance. This was great news, but it meant that our family would have a year in California, while I deployed to Afghanistan, and we would then move to Fort Worth, Texas, where my new command was headquartered.

Over the past year, the fighting had intensified in southern Afghanistan, and we were deploying additional forces to that part of the country. The Marine Corps was tasked to expand its operations in Afghanistan and to create a new NATO command called Regional Command Southwest, a combined US and British command led by a Marine, Major General Richard Mills, who would become the first Marine general to command NATO forces in combat. The command included multiple NATO and non-NATO allies. In Camp Pendleton, we had only a few months to refine our mission and to create a long-term operational plan with supporting tactical plans for southern Afghanistan, all of which had to nest within NATO's overall strategy. We also had to identify, source and train the forces while building and preparing a new leadership team of several hundred Marines and British soldiers.

We began our transition into Afghanistan early in 2010 as the Marines, who were already in-country, were conducting a major combat operation in central Helmand. Simultaneously, we had to create the infrastructure supporting the influx of additional personnel while rotating new units in-country and other units out of country. In business terms, it was like growing from a small, private regional company of a few thousand employees to a large, publicly traded international corporation with over 20,000 new employees from multiple nations in a matter of months all while fighting a determined enemy.

I initially served as the deputy operations officer, responsible for staffing and training the operations team and then, in theater, leading the internal functioning of the operations team. This freed the operations officer to work externally with our allies, sister services and NATO headquarters while orchestrating the overarching combat operations across southwestern Afghanistan. Promoted to colonel in January, I deployed with a small team of about 100 Marines to begin the operational transition. During the transition, I was unexpectedly promoted into the operations officer role. Yet another lesson: always be prepared to fill the next higher position. You never know when you will get the call.

The landing zone at Camp Leatherneck, Helmand, Afghanistan.

View from the back of the Osprey headed into Lashkar Gah, Afghanistan, to meet with British Army counterparts.

En route to a shura ("council") at the Kajaki Dam.

Often a new leader faces a challenge early on, as was the case here. We had recently assumed responsibility for a historically significant area centered on the town of Musa Qala in northern Helmand, which had changed hands many times over the years through intense fighting. We had a Marine battalion establishing a presence in the area when the enemy engaged part of the unit in the afternoon. The Marines soon had the Taliban on the run, capturing weapons and killing some of the fighters in the battle, but the onset of darkness provided the enemy a chance to slip away if the Marines lost contact.

It was a night with low visibility and high winds, making it difficult to see and maneuver. Colonel Paul Kennedy, who would later be promoted to major general, was the regimental commander, and this was one of his units in the fight. Colonel Kennedy had been out with another unit and stopped by our combat operations center on his way back to his command post. We were following the fight, which was nearly an hour away by helicopter, via radio.

As we discussed options, Colonel Kennedy called his commander in the battle, asking, "What do you want to do?"

His unit leader responded that he wanted to press the fight but needed help—more ammunition and evacuation of the wounded. The only option that would enable the Marines to stay in contact was an immediate resupply and casualty evacuation by air, requiring several helicopters. This is a complex operation anytime; however, flying at night into an unknown area in the middle of an ongoing battle compounded by high winds and limited visibility is extremely challenging even for the most experienced pilots.

I called the commander of the aviation combat element and explained the situation. All of his subordinate units had been in combat for months on end and were in the process of rotating out of Afghanistan. I was asking them, days away from going home, to execute one of the most dangerous missions possible.

He replied, "Do you realize what you are asking us to do?"

"Yes," I said, and without hesitation he responded, "We will do it."

The pilots and their crews most likely did not know the Marines who were on the ground fighting that night; however, everyone was in the fight together. It was dangerous. The pilots and their crews selflessly put their lives on the line to help fellow Marines accomplish the mission. They executed the resupply and medical evacuations perfectly, enabling the Marines to fight through the night to mitigate a serious threat. It was an incredible display of character, bravery and selflessness.

Words cannot do justice to what these Marines did on the ground and in the air that night. Most would never know what occurred because it happened regularly. These young people, who were so selflessly committed to each other, their team and their mission, can have the same success in the corporate world. How can such commitment do anything but make an organization better?

Another leadership lesson was how Colonel Kennedy dealt with the issue. This was a small part of his command, maybe 100 men out of several thousand spread across a huge expanse of desert. Colonel Kennedy, the most experienced combat leader in his regiment, turned to his subordinate and asked for his opinion because he was the leader in the fight with the best perspective. The colonel had trained his subordinate leader, trusted him to make the right decision and then supported the decision fully.

I also reflect on the moral courage demonstrated by our aviation commander. He could have, without question, said no and postponed the mission due to the extreme conditions and circumstances, but he knew what was at stake in the bigger picture. As the unit leader, he took full responsibility without hesitation.

On a lighter note, several weeks later we had a young Marine who was part of a patrol in a village. One of the local villagers owned a camel that was having complications delivering its calf. This young Marine recognized what was happening and helped with the delivery. This simple act of humanity helped establish a connection with the local people and created an ally, reinforcing the importance of building relationships as a bridge to solving bigger issues.

CHAPTER 10

"You are having a heart attack."

—ER DOCTOR

THEME: • Being Prepared

I returned from Afghanistan as the school year ended for Alexis and Ward. Once again, as school let out, we began another drive across the country, this time to our new home in Texas. I was assigned to command the 8th Marine Corps District, one of the Marine Corps' six major recruiting commands. The district, headquartered in Fort Worth, covered roughly 28 percent of the country including a large portion of the Rocky Mountain West. It had eight subordinate commands and a reserve component totaling over 6,300 Marines, Marine families and civilians in more than 230 locations across the region.

Getting to Fort Worth required another family move, our third home and the third new school system for Alexis and Ward in thirteen months. The sacrifice military families make to support their service members is incredible; they are the true heroes. Imagine being a child or teenager, having to leave your home and friends to move across the country, knowing as soon as you arrive your dad or mom will be leaving the country for a dangerous job, and not knowing if or when he or she will return. Our military families live with this uncertainty on a regular basis, all without complaint. Their silent and steady service to our country is remarkable and is often overlooked.

The family—Melissa, Alexis, me, and Ward with my parents, Bill and Rudene Studdard.

The first few months after taking command are very busy getting acquainted with your team and learning your new role. Simultaneously, you are assessing the organization's capabilities and how it needs to develop based on its mission requirements. As I met everyone and assessed the unit, I knew that I had a great team of Marines with strong, capable commanders, all of whom were focused on the success of their Marines and their respective commands. We soon hit our stride with the entire organization functioning smoothly.

We settled into our new home and integrated into the local community, and, before we knew it, we were two years into the three-year tour. My replacement was selected, which normally happens a year in advance, and it was time to decide what was next for our family. During the last year of a tour, we always gathered around the kitchen table for a family meeting. First, we decided whether to do another tour, and if we all agreed to keep going, we discussed the options for my next assignment. This discussion was like all the rest; Melissa, Alexis and Ward were fully supportive of another tour.

After the kids went to bed, Melissa and I revisited the topic. Several extenuating circumstances made this decision a bit different from previous ones. My next tour would most likely be in a staff role, which I did not relish after being in command. Ward was a year away from high school, and we were acutely aware of how hard moving to three high schools in three years had been on Alexis. I loved everything about being a Marine, but I also knew that at some point it ends for every Marine. If I was ever going to retire, this was the best time for our family. Ward could attend one high school, and I was still young enough to have a second career. After much deliberation and prayer, I prepared to turn in my retirement papers.

I flew to our higher headquarters in San Diego, California, and met with my commanding general, Brigadier General Dan Yoo, who told me he was not going to submit my retirement request. I was taken aback that he was not supportive. However, as we talked, I knew he was doing me a favor. Regardless of my next role (I had not spoken with my monitor, whose job it was to make assignments, because I did not want the possibility of an exciting opportunity to cloud my judgment), I cherished being a Marine and really did not want to retire. Furthermore, I did not have a plan. I had no idea what I wanted to do, and we as a family didn't know where we wanted to live.

I realized I had been somewhat cavalier and that retiring made little sense. After our conversation, I called my monitor to see what assignments were available, and, to my surprise, he presented me with an opportunity to return to Afghanistan. I would be serving with two Marines for whom I had enormous respect and with whom I had worked closely in the Pentagon and in Afghanistan—Lieutenant

General Joe Dunford, who later became the 19th Chairman of the Joint Chiefs of Staff, and Major General Jody Osterman , who would later command the First Marine Expeditionary Force as a Lieutenant General. This was an operational role; I would lead the planning, coordination and execution of operations across the country. I felt as if I had dodged a bullet by not having the retirement papers forwarded. I was on top of the world, and, more importantly, Melissa and the kids were on board.

Lieutenant General Joe Dunford promoting me to colonel in Camp Pendleton, California, prior to my deployment to Afghanistan.

We were discussing family logistics for the deployment when I received word that I had been selected to serve as part of a group of senior officers on a promotion board in Quantico, Virginia. The board would meet in the late fall for about a month. I had participated in selection boards before and knew that we would be working straight through, including weekends, until the board completed its function. Serving on a board is similar to jury duty with all board members sequestered and working together in a closed room for the duration.

The Saturday of my departure was like any Saturday at home. We were up early, Melissa prepared a big breakfast, and we ate together. It was so good that I enjoyed an extra cup of coffee before departing for the airport. I traveled frequently, and when I left for the airport from the headquarters, my driver, Sergeant Dustin Andrews, would drop me off. On this occasion, since I was leaving from home, Melissa was taking me. En route, we made a quick stop to pick up a bottle of Maalox. I had too much coffee and thought a swig of Maalox would help—it didn't. Melissa suggested we stop by the emergency room at Baylor Medical Center in Fort Worth, which was on our way to the airport. Of course, I said no; she persisted, and again I said no. She then played her trump card by saying, "You know if you are sick, you may make the other board members sick as well. You still have plenty of time to catch your flight or even take a later one." With that pearl of wisdom, she pulled off the interstate and up to the emergency room entrance, and we went inside.

I thought that early on a Saturday morning in Fort Worth there would be plenty of cowboys in line waiting for stitches after a fun Friday night. A long line would give me a perfect excuse to leave. To my surprise, the waiting room was empty. I was immediately triaged and sent to an exam room to wait for the doctor. At this point, I thought that there was still hope. Without other visible patients, perhaps they would see me quickly and send me on my way with enough time to make my flight.

Just as I began to think this could still work out, the door burst open and the doctor rushed in, pushing Melissa aside, followed by several nurses, all of whom moved with a sense of urgency. My expression must have given me away; he answered my unasked question: "You are having a heart attack!"

In that split second, everything slowed down. I thought that there had to be a mistake. Some old guy was in another room having a heart attack and needed help, and the medical team was in the wrong room—this could never happen to me. Didn't these people know that I was a Marine? Didn't they know that earlier in the week I completed my annual Combat Fitness Test with a perfect score? Didn't they know I had never missed a day of work?

The flurry of activity snapped me back into the moment. The next few hours passed in controlled chaos as the medical team worked on me. The crazy thing is that I did not feel very bad or hurt very much. I kept thinking any minute they would come in and tell me that everything was all right. I felt terrible for Melissa; all she could do was stand by my side while the team worked. I imagined how helpless I would have felt if the roles were reversed. Once everything was under control, I was admitted to the hospital. It turned out that the medical team was right, and I was wrong.

While Melissa called the kids and the rest of our family to let them know what was happening, I made calls to the head of the promotion board and to my sergeant major, JB Edwards. Each of these conversations was surreal; never in a million years did I think I would have a heart attack.

Over the next forty-eight hours, I was tested, poked, prodded, and violated in every imaginable way. The episode is a bit comical now; however, at the time, it was anything but funny. By Monday morning, the medical team completed the procedures and released me with a series of follow-up appointments lined up through Christmas.

Melissa took me straight to my headquarters so I could speak with my staff. After talking with everyone, I went to my office and closed the door. I knew that I had a decision to make. I was not sure what would come next; I did not know if I would be allowed to stay in the Marine Corps, but I knew that I certainly would not be going back to Afghanistan. If I were allowed to stay in the Corps, I would most likely be relegated to a desk job.

I didn't want to be a straphanger, and I definitely did not want to turn into some fat old colonel marking time. The decision was clear; I would retire. I walked downstairs and asked my personnel officer to stop by my office to help me with my paperwork. While the decision was easy mentally, it was difficult emotionally given the recent soul-searching and subsequent decision to stay in the Marine Corps only to have everything change so abruptly.

I was honored to be a Marine; it exceeded any expectation I could have imagined. Serving beside some of the most amazing people on earth has been a lifelong gift. I had truly lived a dream and was at peace with the way forward with one small exception. I did not have a back-up plan, and to make matters worse, I should have known better. Whether you are at the tactical, operational, or strategic level, there is a basic warfighting principle that I had taught and practiced professionally—have a back-up plan.

At the tactical level, I prepared primary, alternate and supplemental positions, and at operational and strategic levels I prepared branches and sequels. No matter what they are called, they are essentially back-up plans. I had practiced this my entire professional career. Unfortunately, in my personal life I did not have a back-up plan, which was now abundantly clear.

CHAPTER 11

*"No matter how bad or chaotic the situation is,
there is always time to think."*

—COLONEL BOB FAWCETT

THEME: • Charting a New Path • Considering Values

December quickly turned into January, then February. In addition to preparing the command for turnover to my successor, I had multiple follow-up medical appointments as well as all the retirement requirements. As time flew by, I realized I had done little over the years to prepare for a career after the Marine Corps. I did not know what I wanted to do other than be in charge, which I have since learned is not a job description in Corporate America. Like many people with my background, leading a team or an organization is one of my strengths; however, I did not have an industry, a company or a specific role that I wanted to target. I did not know what opportunities were out there, and I certainly did not know how to find them. Moreover, our family had lived in many different places, and Melissa turned every duty station into a home. We felt that we could live anywhere and be happy. This sounds good until you have unlimited choices, and then it can be a challenge.

Although I had not actively started looking for a second career, I did have a huge advantage working in my favor—American Corporate Partners (ACP). Soon after taking command of the 8th District, my supply officer, Captain Charlie Lichtenberger, who was retiring, stopped by my office late one afternoon to discuss our supply account. As we were talking, he told me about a mentorship program he was participating in through ACP. The yearlong program paired corporate leaders with service members who were exiting the service to help facilitate a smooth transition by leveraging their corporate experience. Charlie went on to explain how his ACP mentor was helping him navigate his new path into Corporate America. As I listened, I realized that in addition to being a great resource for transitioning service members, the ACP mentors could also be an additional leadership resource.

My subordinate commanders led large, dispersed organizations and faced the same issues that traditional business leaders faced, including meeting monthly sales quotas, staffing and training a large organization, managing budget constraints, and maximizing advertising and marketing opportunities. After our conversation, I called ACP founder, Sidney Goodfriend, in New York and asked if we could pair some of his mentors with my leaders to expand their leadership repertoires. I thought that connecting Marine leaders with local corporate leaders would be a good experience for both and that it would also strengthen our local relationships. Mr. Goodfriend agreed, and we paired several leaders with good results.

Charlie's success with his ACP mentor encouraged other transitioning Marines to join the program. Two years later, when it was time for me to begin the retirement process, I knew that an ACP mentor was the place to start. Burnis J. Hebert, President, Occidental Chemical Corporation, was my initial mentor, and I am forever grateful for the time and effort he invested in me. I was in uncharted waters, and B. J. helped me immeasurably with resume preparation and advice on navigating corporate politics, and through the ongoing professional guidance he has graciously provided since.

Melissa and I began discussing options regarding location. We were open to moving most anywhere for an interesting job opportunity but decided that we should also explore opportunities in Georgia where we both still had family ties. There was one small problem; we had a strong network of people across the country except in Georgia since we had not lived there in twenty-five years. ACP came to the rescue and transferred me to a new mentor in Atlanta, Todd Chapman, who could help me network and identify local opportunities.

Life moved at double time. Although I had prepared a resume and we were considering a general location, I had not given due diligence to the type of career or industry that I wanted to pursue. Thankfully, at this point I received a call from a Fortune 100 bank asking if I was interested in discussing a role in New York as part of their international banking business. Saying yes was easy, as I had no other prospects. Having never interviewed for a corporate position, I knew I should get some help preparing for the interview. I called Todd, and he graciously agreed to help me, suggesting that I fly to Georgia so we could work together in person.

Todd was an executive at The Home Depot, and we decided to meet at one of their stores in Atlanta. We began with a tour of the store, and as we walked the aisles and talked with the associates, I was immediately aware of the pride they had in their store and their company. I saw and felt a sense of camaraderie. I did not know what to expect, but this level of ownership and personal connection struck me as different, and in a good way. Completing the store walk, we went into the conference room and began work.

Midway through our interview preparation, Todd excused himself to take a phone call. I noticed a circular diagram painted on the wall and went over to investigate. To my surprise, the circle was The Home Depot value wheel, and around it were the eight Home Depot values—taking care of our people, doing the right thing, respect for all people, entrepreneurial spirit, giving back, excellent customer service, building strong relationships, and creating shareholder value.

The diagram made me think of the Marine Corps core values— honor, courage and commitment. The words were different, but the values hit home. In essence, it was saying to do what was right even if no one was looking, absolutely what we followed as Marines. Even more intriguing was the image next to the value wheel, an inverted pyramid with the CEO on the bottom and other layers of leadership stacked on top with front-line associates and customers at the very top. Again, this spoke to me. It was the Marine Corps leadership model—leaders eat last—articulated in civilian terms. Todd returned and we finished the interview preparation, yet my thoughts kept returning to the value wheel and the inverted pyramid.

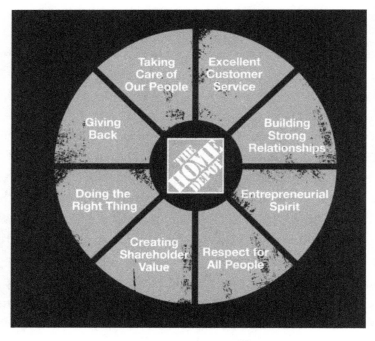

The Home Depot Value Wheel.

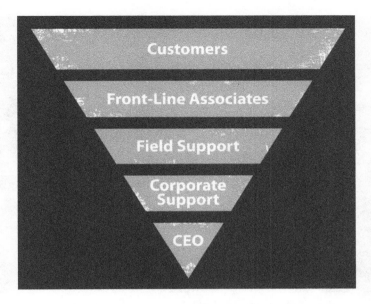

The Home Depot Inverted (Leadership) Pyramid.

A few days later, I flew to New York and began the interview process. After the evening reception, I went back to my hotel room. Sitting on the edge of the bed, I took off my shoes and looked down at the hustle and bustle in Times Square.

I was intrigued by The Home Depot values; the images of the value wheel and inverted pyramid kept coming to mind. I was so focused on getting a job that I had not taken the time to consider values, either professionally or personally, as part of the equation. Of course, I knew better. When I checked in to The Basic School as an instructor, our commanding officer, Colonel Bob Fawcett, told me during our initial meeting that regardless of what I was teaching the lieutenants, there was one thing he always wanted me to reinforce. He told me that no matter how bad or chaotic the situation was, there was always time to think; even if only for a split second, there was always time to think, and I needed to convey this to the lieutenants. Sitting in that hotel room, I realized I had not taken time to think about values in relation to my post–Marine Corps career.

Discussing tactics before a patrol with Colonel Bob Fawcett, who taught me there is always time to think.

I knew I wanted to work with a reputable company. My primary consideration at the time was finding a good job that would provide for our family, and that was the extent of it. I was not looking at the job situation holistically. When I took the time to think, I recognized there were other dynamics I needed to consider. Our daughter, Alexis, would soon be on her way to college, so our decision on where to live and what to do career-wise really did not affect her. However, Melissa and I saw how challenging it was for her to move to three different high schools in three years. Arlington, Virginia; Oceanside, California; Aledo, Texas—all were vastly different. Alexis was a trooper, but it was hard to move so much at such an important time in her life.

Our son, Ward, who would soon be going to high school, was the typical Marine kid and loved everything outdoors. We often laughed that he never learned to tie his shoes because he was always barefoot while searching for outdoor adventure with the other kids on the base. Ward was definitely not one to be confined to concrete or asphalt. Finally, our parents were aging, and due to the location of our duty stations, we had not spent much time with them over the past twenty-five years.

Professionally, serving in the Marine Corps was a source of pride. The institution is very reputable and is held in high esteem by both the public and militaries around the world. It prides itself on intangible qualities that are important to me, such as ethics, character, and moral courage. Although I did not know the path I would choose, I knew that I needed to align with an organization with professional values akin to mine.

The day after the evening reception was full of interviews with multiple leaders from the bank. As the day closed, the last interviewer asked me if I wanted the job. I knew when I paused before answering that this was not the right fit for me; I thanked him and said no. We shook hands and I departed. The decision felt good on the elevator ride down to the lobby, and the positive feeling continued until I stepped onto the street.

Then it hit me like a punch to the gut. I had turned down the only professional job offer I ever had, and to make matters worse, I did not have any other prospects. This was a great job, with a great company, in a great location, and I had just said no. What had I done? Remembering Colonel Fawcett's talk and taking the time to think made me realize that despite the positives about the job and the company, it was not the right fit at the right time for our family.

I told Todd about the interview, and he asked if I had considered The Home Depot. I told him no and explained that Melissa was the one in the family with home improvement experience. With me being away from home so much, she took care of anything that needed to be fixed or upgraded. He told me home improvement experience was not a prerequisite and described some of the opportunities within The Home Depot.

Shortly after my return from New York, I turned the command over to my successor. I had accrued leave and used it to begin my job search in earnest while waiting for my official retirement date. Over the next two months, Todd arranged for me to meet with different field leaders to learn more about the company, and I liked what I saw. As I began networking in earnest over the summer, additional opportunities materialized; however, the values and leadership I saw at The Home Depot during my field visits kept drawing me back.

As the summer closed, Alexis departed for school while Melissa, Ward and I packed up and moved to Georgia. Soon after, I accepted an offer from The Home Depot, and we settled on a start date in the early fall.

CHAPTER 12

"Would you put them in your role in Afghanistan?"

—MELISSA STUDDARD

THEME: · Change and Growth

I began my second career as a co-manager of a large, high-volume Home Depot store in Atlanta. I was transitioning into the next phase of life as a civilian. I knew there would be change, but I did not anticipate the magnitude of the change.

I had never given transition much thought. It happened when you moved into a new role or assumed a new command. Transition was something that occurred routinely along a predictable timeline, but as time passed I became aware that the move back into civilian life was far more than transitional. It was transformational.

As I was rehearsing a new class on transition for a group of newly promoted leaders, it dawned on me that we are in a state of transition every day. Physically, we begin as infants and grow into toddlers, teenagers and adults. Our bodies are in an ongoing state of transition. Professionally, we start with chores at home and move into part-time jobs followed by full-time jobs, which often turn into long-term careers. Throughout our working lives, we are constantly learning and growing, i.e., transitioning. Hundreds if not thousands of people intersect our personal lives. The length of these relationships varies over the course of a lifetime, but the vast majority are transitory in nature. The one constant in our lives is that we are always in a state of transition or perpetual change.

I began to see transformation as an intense period of change and growth, far more comprehensive than the routine and frequent transitions I had encountered to date. I, along with every other Marine or service member, had been through a transformation before. We all transformed from civilians into soldiers, sailors, airmen, or Marines. However, the initial transformation was different because we went through the process with our peers. Each service supplied its own team of friendly human resource specialists called drill instructors to help guide us through the transformation while instilling the respective service culture. At our first duty station, our unit continued assisting with our transformation. Exiting the service and transforming back into a civilian is different. It is often an individual experience, and unless one has a strong personal network, it is easy to become isolated thinking you are the only one having this experience.

This transformational epiphany hit me several months into my new career. I came home from work, and Melissa could tell immediately that something was bothering me. My frustration had been building for a few weeks and must have shown on my face and in my body language.

She asked me what was wrong, and I said to her, "I'm not sure I can do this."

She said, "What do you mean?"

I replied, "I'm not sure I can do this job."

Being a Marine's spouse, she quickly put things into perspective and pointed out that I gladly accepted Home Depot's offer and was in a highly sought-after role in a perfect location.

She was right, of course, but I thought she did not fully understand the scope of my frustration, so I began to explain. Just a few months ago, I was an active duty Marine colonel responsible for over 6,300 Marines, sailors and civilians twenty-four hours a day, seven days a week. I had a seventy-plus-person staff, which allowed me to discharge my duties across more than a quarter of the country. I was the recipient of the professional courtesies extended to senior officers in every branch of the service. Accountable for thousands of people, millions of dollars in equipment and facilities, and a multi-million dollar operating budget, I enjoyed tremendous autonomy. Throughout my career, I thrived on responsibility, and every role in which I served provided that and more.

I pointed out that we had approximately 200 associates who were a part of our store, but less than 50 of them actually worked in the store on any given day. I reminded Melissa that as a platoon commander twenty-five years ago, I was accountable for double the amount of people we had working in the store, and had deployed with them globally on multiple occasions as well as leading them in combat. I finished by telling her that I had more responsibility, authority and autonomy as a young Marine lieutenant than I did in my current role.

She patiently listened; I expected her to agree and to share my frustrations—I was wrong. Melissa took a deep breath and said, "Ok, now let me ask you a question. Would you take any executive out of The Home Depot and put them into your role in Afghanistan?"

I thought for a moment, knowing that I had already met extremely bright and capable leaders who had the intangibles to be successful in any organization. Yet, despite having the character, intellect and leadership skills to fulfill the role, they did not have the depth of institutional knowledge or the breadth of warfighting experience to immediately step in and succeed on day one.

I responded with "No."

She looked at me and said, "There is your answer."

I knew she was right. I had to learn the business in depth. More importantly, I had to understand and experience the culture. Most importantly, I needed to learn the people. I acknowledged that I had to take a step back in responsibility in order to prepare for a step forward in the future.

It is counterintuitive to think that a job with less responsibility and increased pay is anything but good. However, as I have discovered through many conversations with fellow veterans, diminished responsibility is the most common point of frustration.

Soon after, I learned that taking a step back in responsibility also requires a degree of humility.

I was in the store, and an associate came to me and said, "Ted, we have a problem."

Finally, a problem to solve! I could not wait to hear what it was. My mind raced ahead; perhaps it was a shipping problem or an upset customer or we were about to get a short-notice executive walk (The Home Depot version of an inspection).

His comment caught me by surprise: "There is a problem in the bathroom."

Disappointed, I asked him to let our custodial team know. He informed me they were gone for the day, so I said, "Let's go check it out." He let me know that the restroom in question was the family restroom. As I set out in this direction, he stopped me, saying he had other priorities, and quickly walked away.

Although I am not a handyman, I thought I could fix whatever problem we had. Then I opened the door.

The sights and smells were something to behold. I have been a few places and have seen a few things, but this was special and not in a good way. The upside was that I worked in The Home Depot, and I was able to fashion a civilian version of a MOPP suit, which is a military acronym for a mission oriented protective posture overgarment worn in hazardous environments to protect against chemical, radiological, biological or nuclear contaminants. Armed with a bottle of Clorox and an industrial-strength plunger, I went to work. If there was a silver lining to this cloud, it was having the opportunity to exercise my entire Marine Corps vocabulary as I plunged and cleaned.

I am absolutely not above cleaning toilets, and as a Marine private, I cleaned many; however, as a Marine colonel, I definitely did not clean toilets. This proved to be a great lesson. I was starting over in a new organization in a completely new role, and I had to get used to it. I knew that I was in a period of transformation—a period of intense change and intense growth.

Teaching leadership at Home Depot University.

I spent over a year learning the ropes in several different stores, which proved to be invaluable. Store managers Bobby Cole and

Daniel Opene were extraordinary teachers and helped me beyond measure. Working in the store opened a dream opportunity for me—teaching leadership at Home Depot University. Although I had been in leadership positions my entire adult life, I had to know the details of store operations; I had to know the challenges that our field leaders and associates faced every day; and I had to understand the cultural context in which it all happened in order to be an effective leadership teacher at Home Depot University.

Without the time in the store, I would not have been given this opportunity. Serving as a leadership instructor allowed me to interact with many leaders across the company, including those in our merchandising organization. As the merchandising execution team grew to over 26,000 associates, I was offered a newly created role—divisional staffing manager for the western division. The field operational experience in the stores provided an opportunity to learn the training component for a Fortune 25 company and subsequently the staffing component for this company of over 400,000 associates. Taking a step back in responsibility led to another step forward.

Melissa knew I had to transform to learn a new business, to learn new people and to learn a new culture. I was blessed to have her by my side, helping me navigate the process.

ACKNOWLEDGEMENTS

I would like to thank the people who provided the help necessary to complete this book, starting with my family, Melissa, Alexis and Ward Studdard, all of whom have given me far more than I can ever return.

I am forever grateful for all the Marines that I was privileged to serve alongside, with a special thank-you to the Marines of B 1/12 and the Marines of RS Nashville for all you taught me.

Thank you to my team at Limitless Creative, John Watson and Matt Uberseder along with Hemda Mizrahi, who dedicated the extra effort to make this work a success.

Thank you to the associates at The Home Depot who welcomed me into a new team.

Thank you to all who have provided proofreads along with input and insight, to include Brent Wood, Leo Smith and Bonnie Ogden.

It has been a pleasure working with John Koehler and his team of professionals at Koehler Books Publishing.

APPENDIX 1

MARINE CORPS RANK STRUCTURE AND RANK INSIGNIA

ENLISTED

PRIVATE (E-1)	**PRIVATE** **FIRST CLASS** (E-2)	**LANCE** **CORPORAL** (E-3)	**CORPORAL** (E-4)	**SERGEANT** (E-5)	**STAFF** **SERGEANT** (E-6)

WARRANT OFFICER

(Red and Gold Bar)	*(Red and Gold Bars)*	*(Red and Silver Bar)*	*(Red and Silver Bars)*	*(Silver and Red Center)*
WARRANT **OFFICER** (W-1)	**CHIEF** **WARRANT** **OFFICER 2** (CWO2)	**CHIEF** **WARRANT** **OFFICER 3** (CWO3)	**CHIEF** **WARRANT** **OFFICER 4** (CWO4)	**CHIEF** **WARRANT** **OFFICER 5** (CWO5)

COMMISSIONED OFFICER

  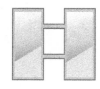

(Gold)			*(Gold)*	
2ND LT (O-1)	**1ST LT** (O-2)	**CAPTAIN** (O-3)	**MAJOR** (O-4)	**LIEUTENANT** **COLONEL** (O-5)

| **GUNNERY SERGEANT** (E-7) | **MASTER SERGEANT** (E-8) | **FIRST SERGEANT** (E-8) | **MASTER GUNNERY SERGEANT** (E-9) | **SERGEANT MAJOR** (E-9) | **SERGEANT MAJOR OF THE MARINE CORPS** (E-9) |

| **COLONEL** (O-6) | **BRIGADIER GENERAL** (O-7) | **MAJOR GENERAL** (O-8) | **LIEUTENANT GENERAL** (O-9) | **GENERAL** (O-10) |

APPENDIX 2

Leader's Rank	Type of Command	Size of Command
Second Lieutenant	Platoon	40–100
First Lieutenant	Platoon	40–100
Captain	Company / Battery (Artillery)	150–300
Lieutenant Colonel	Battalion	500–1000
Colonel	Regiment	3000–4000
Major General	Division	15,000–20,000
Lieutenant General	Marine Expeditionary Force	30,000–50,000

APPENDIX 3

MILITARY TAKEAWAYS FOR
TRANSITION AND TRANSFORMATION

- When deciding on next steps, prioritize what is most important to you and your family, which in turn will help align your post-service career search and focus your decisions. Think through your values and then consider the following:

  1. Location—Is there a specific location or region where you want to live?
  2. Company—Is there a specific company you want to join?
  3. Role/Title—Is there a specific position you want?
  4. Industry Type—Is there a specific industry type for you?
  5. Professional Growth—Do you want to pursue a career with a company that provides opportunity for upward mobility? Are you willing to relocate for growth opportunities?
  6. How hard you want to work—What is the level of commitment that you and your family are willing to put into your second career?

Once you have considered your priorities above, the scope of your transition and subsequent transformation will become much clearer and easier to manage.

- Determine how long you can go financially without working. This directs how long you can search and when you need to say "yes" to an opportunity.

- Be prepared to articulate the unique value that you bring. Sell your intangibles, such as your ability to take on an unfamiliar role, learn it quickly, and execute at a high level. Appendix 4 highlights many of the intangibles that veterans bring to the workplace.

- Don't wait for your heart attack. Have a back-up plan.

- Don't wait to consider your values. Take time to think and align with an organization whose professional values synchronize with yours.

- Don't be afraid to take a step back in responsibility. It can lead to a great leap forward.

- Exiting the service is transformational; it is an intense period of growth and change required to learn a new business, to learn new people and to learn a new culture.

APPENDIX 4

C orporations have an opportunity to leverage the experience of our veteran community. Often a short-term investment in teaching the details of your business yields an exceptional long-term return.

Our senior military leaders comprise a small, but extremely capable portion, of the overall veteran workforce. Through their years of global service they have successfully taken on many new and complex roles. Furthermore, they are life-long learners who readily adapt to change and new environments.

The benefits of incorporating senior military leaders into your boardroom include:

- World-wide experience leading large organizations with a culturally diverse workforce. They know how to build and maintain teams that focus on commonalities vice differences.

- Extensive formal leadership training combined with years of practical experience, which they can use to help create internal leadership and mentoring programs that increase retention and develop bench strength.

- Proficiency in solving unique, complex problems using an inclusive team-based approach. Their perspective often reveals business gaps while providing new ideas and solutions.

- Creating and maintaining a positive culture anchored to an ethical foundation is a common denominator that enabled these leaders to advance in their respective service. Their experience is beneficial to companies that are growing rapidly and to companies that are making new acquisitions.

- Effective communicators who are able to connect at all levels across a large organization. A key ingredient to their success was creating and communicating their vision in such a way that it resonated with all. Additionally, these leaders are accustomed to representing the organization publicly and are adept at negotiating for the organization.

APPENDIX 5

LEADERSHIP TAKEAWAYS

- A few minutes spent mentoring or sharing life experiences can provide a lifelong foundation.
- Moral courage, the willingness to do what is right regardless of circumstance, is critical to leadership.
- Trust is earned. The leader's reaction to a bad situation will either quickly build trust or quickly erode trust.
- Mistakes will happen; how you deal with mistakes often matters far more than the mistake.
- Ensure that team members understand the impact of their actions, and hold them accountable, regardless of their role or title.
- Consistency + Accountability = Sustainability
- Organizations often arbitrarily determine that they have achieved success and fail to see the need to improve. Complacency kills in combat and in business.
- Leadership teams are most effective when they leverage their individual strengths.
- Take the time to mentor your subordinates. Often the investment that provides the highest return is the investment a leader makes in one-on-one time with junior leaders.

- Teach, empower, and trust.
- Use every opportunity to prepare your people for future, more complex roles.
- Leaders have the unwritten responsibility to pay it forward.
- The best leaders provide ongoing opportunities for their subordinates to gain experience and grow.
- Confident leaders:
  ○ Provide opportunity to subordinates.
  ○ Stand by their team in a crisis.
  ○ Share ownership.
  ○ Know their job.
  ○ Demonstrate humility.
- Sharing ownership turns "my" team into "our" team.
- Physical courage is important; moral courage is imperative.
- Leaders also need feedback for their own growth.
- Incredible results happen when a team owns its mission.
- When individuals and subordinate organizations succeed, the parent organization succeeds as a by-product.
- Bloom where you are planted.
- Finding commonality helps build relationships, which in turns creates a foundation to solve problems.
- Clearly communicating your team's mission and the results it needs to achieve enables junior leaders to make sound, time-sensitive decisions.
- Ensure that subordinate leaders understand how your training program is linked to the team's success (i.e., explain the "why" behind your training").
- Understanding culture is equally important whether it is working country-to-country or business-to-business.
- Whether creating a positive culture, changing a toxic culture or integrating a new team into the larger enterprise, if the culture (i.e., the foundation) is sound at the beginning, everything built on it will stand.

- Leaders are responsible for building and maintaining organizational relationships.
- Personal relationships provide venues for solving problems outside the spotlight and can help mitigate problems before they grow.
- Teach and then trust the people on the scene to make the right decisions.
- The leader has ultimate responsibility for everything the team does or fails to do.
- Have a back-up plan.